Volume 10

MODERN FIGHTING AIRCRAFT
TORNADO

An Arco Aviation Book

Published by

PRENTICE HALL PRESS

New York

A Salamander Book

Credits

An Arco Aviation Book

Published by Prentice Hall Press
A Division of Simon & Schuster, Inc.
Simon & Schuster Building
Rockefeller Center
1230 Avenue of the Americas
New York, New York 10020

1 2 3 4 5 6 7 8 9 10

Library of Congress Cataloging-in-Publication Data
Main entry under title:

Tornado.

(Modern Fighting Aircraft; v. 10)
"An Arco Aviation book"
1. Tornado (Jet fighter plane) I. Series.
UG1242.F5T67   1986   623.74′64   85-23323
ISBN 0-13-925504-4

All correspondence concerning the content
of this book should be addressed to
Salamander Books Ltd.,
52 Bedford Row, London WC1R 4LR,
United Kingdom.

This book may not be sold outside the
United States of America and Canada.

Project Manager: Ray Bonds

Editor: Bernard Fitzsimons

Designer: Nick Buzzard

Diagrams: TIGA © Salamander Books Ltd.

Jacket: Terry Hadler

Colour profiles: Mark Franklin,
© Salamander Books Ltd, and
© Pilot Press Ltd.

Cutaway drawings: © Pilot Press Ltd.

Three-view drawings: Mike Badrocke
© Salamander Books Ltd.

Contents

Acknowledgements

Author

It is impossible to write a book on
Tornado without acknowledging a debt
to Bill Gunston. For many years a one-
man Tornado industry, he has been the
most active author in the field,
documenting the type's early history and
development in painstaking detail.

Thanks are also due to Panavia, David
Kamiya of British Aerospace, Aeritalia,
MBB, Turbo-Union, Rolls-Royce and all
those whose contributions are detailed
above and in the picture credits at the
end of the book.

Finally, the chapter on Operational
Employment was contributed by Mike
Spick.

Doug Richardson is a defence journalist
specializing in the fields of aviation,
guided missiles and electronics. After an
electronics R&D career encompassing
such diverse areas as radar, electronic
warfare, rocket engine control systems,
computers, automatic test equipment
and missile trials, he switched to
technical journalism. He has been
Defence Editor of *Flight International*
and Editor of the journals *Military
Technology and Economics* and
Defence Materiel, and his previous work
for Salamander includes *The Illustrated
Encyclopedia of Modern Warplanes*
(1982), *An Illustrated Survey of the
West's Modern Fighters* (1984) and *An
Illustrated Guide to the Techniques and
Equipment of Electronic Warfare* (1985),
as well as two earlier volumes in this
series, *F-16 Fighting Falcon* (1983) and
F-4 Phantom II (1984, with Mike Spick).

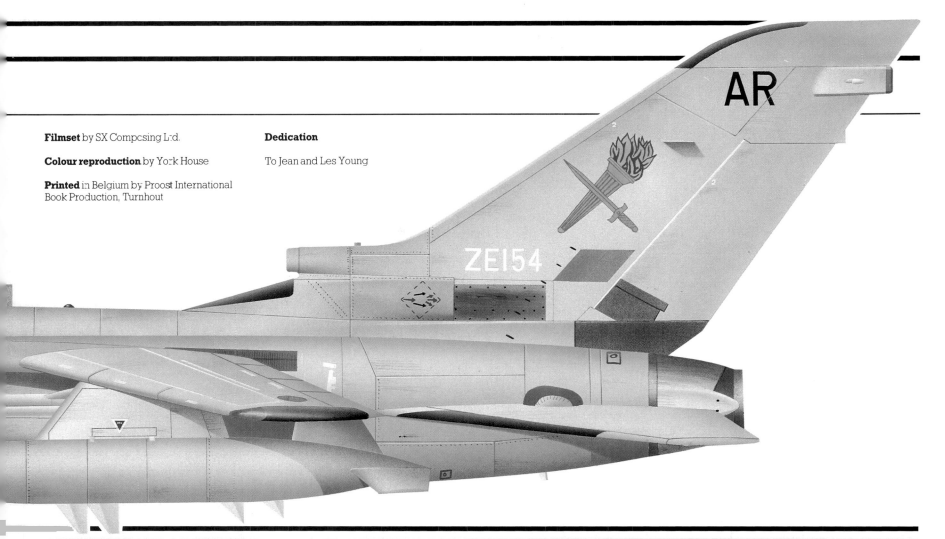

Filmset by SX Compcsing Lnd.

Colour reproduction by York House

Printed in Belgium by Proost International
Book Production, Turnhout

Dedication

To Jean and Les Young

Introduction

For the Panavia partners, Tornado was a challenge of massive proportions, none of the collaborating nations being overburdened with supersonic fighter design expertise. The UK had only managed to design, fly and deploy a single type, the BAC Lightning – an aircraft originally conceived as a research tool back in the days when King George VI was still on the throne and the RAF's front-line fighter pilots could only dream of the day when swept-wing replacements might reach the squadrons. West German and Italian supersonic fighter experience was limited to having licence-built the F-104.

In theory, the product of the MRCA programme could have been little more than a reinvented F-105 Thunderchief: instead, the partners took the bold step of combining variable geometry, an advanced turbofan of novel configuration and the latest generation of avionics to create a STOL fighter far excelling the F-4 Phantom without being much bigger than an F-16 Fighting Falcon. In retrospect, the decision seems almost foolhardy, and the result could have been the biggest aeronautical disaster since the US Navy's F-111B, but it ended

up as the hardest-hitting tactical fighter in the world. The USAF's F-111D/E/F fighters may have a greater range, but the RAF's success in bombing competitions has shown the Panavia aircraft's unsurpassed ability to place ordnance on target.

This level of performance must be paid for, so many prospective export customers have shopped elsewhere for their next-generation fighters, selecting cheaper designs less closely configured to the strike role and better suited to the interception mission. Only in the Middle East has Tornado found favour, being adopted by nations which face Israel's battle-honed air force or the sophisticated F-14 Tomcats flown by aircrew under the command of the Ayatollah Khomeini.

Tornado seems assured of a long career with the five nations to have ordered the type, and with dedicated electronic warfare and reconnaissance versions planned for Luftwaffe and RAF service, and mid-life updates already under consideration, this book can only serve as a progress report and a pointer toward the future. Twenty years or more will pass before the final chapter of the Tornado story can be written.

Development

In the late 1960s, five NATO nations agreed to collaborate on the development of a new fighter to meet the needs of their respective air arms. By the time the planned Multirole Combat Aircraft (MRCA) finally entered front-line service in 1982 as the Panavia Tornado, the number of partners had fallen to three, and the programme had set the unenviable record of having the greatest ever interval between go-ahead and first flight, as well as the longest time from first flight to entry into service. Despite these delays, the resulting aircraft is probably the best example of a multi-purpose warplane since the Luftwaffe's last Ju 88 went to the breakers back in 1945.

Above: Following the cancellation of the BAC TSR-2 and the RAF's F-111K order, the UK teamed with France to work on the short-lived Anglo-French Variable Geometry (AFVG) design. When France pulled out, the UK kept the project alive as the UKVG, represented in this model.

Tornado is the most combat-effective interdiction/strike aircraft in service with the air forces of the West, and almost certainly in the world. If forced to risk life and limb in a combat sortie into heavily-defended airspace, the author would sooner tackle the assignment in Tornado than in any other front-line type of the mid-1980s.

Tornado is no all-embracing jack of all trades – it cannot match the dogfight manoeuvrability of the F-14 and F-15, the long range of the F-111, or the short take-off and landing performance of the Harrier and AV-8B. But no other aircraft can match Tornado's combination of small size, long range, and high speed in low-level terrain-following flight. In these respects, the Panavia aircraft is unquestionably unique.

The Tornado programme began back in the 1960s, a time of crisis for the aircraft industries of the world. The first generation of Mach 2 fighters had been successfully developed and deployed on both sides of the Atlantic and in the Soviet Union, but the West now faced the massive cost of developing the next generation of fighters and strike aircraft – warplanes able to survive and fight in the face of the growing threat posed by surface-to-air and air-to-air missiles.

No aircraft industry was more racked by changes of plan and cancellation than that of the UK. By the early summer of 1965 the British Aircraft Corporation (BAC) had spent six years developing the TSR-2 long-range supersonic STOL strike aircraft to meet the RAF's Canberra-replacement requirement GOR.339, only to see the project cancelled by a recently-elected Labour government which seemed to have an almost pathological hatred of the British aircraft industry.

Minister of Defence in the new government was Denis Healey. Considered a political moderate by the stan-dards of the 1980s, he promptly earned himself the epithet of "The Mad Axeman" back in 1963 by launching into a series of aircraft cancellations – the Hawker Siddeley P.1154 V/STOL fighter, its supporting Hawker Siddeley HS.681 STOL transport, and finally TSR-2 itself.

The events of the next few years were to verge on comedy, providing an object lesson on how not to run a defence policy or an aircraft industry. In the short term the RAF was allowed to order US warplanes, the F-4 Phantom and the C-130 Hercules being selected to replace the P.1154 and HS.681. Having cancelled TSR-2, the British Government turned to the only other Western aircraft in the same performance class, the General Dynamics F-111, and an option was duly taken out on the GD warplane.

Purchases of US aircraft were seen as a stop-gap measure: in the longer term, the UK would develop its military aircraft in collaboration with other Western European nations. The chosen partner was France, and the two nations – already linked by the Concorde super-sonic airliner project – now began further ventures.

On May 17, 1965, Britain and France signed a Memorandum of Understanding covering the development and manufacture of a new supersonic strike trainer by Breguet and BAC, and committing both partners to "... examine a variable-geometry aircraft for the middle and late 1970s ... to formulate technical specifications ... with the intention of entering upon a joint pro-gramme ..."

The first aircraft covered by the agreement was what was to become the Jaguar fighter-bomber, now in service with the air forces of the UK, France, India, Oman, Ecuador and Nigeria, and the two partners agreed to order a total of 400. Such a large-scale purchase was a novel experience for the British aircraft industry and the hidebound British procurement system with which it traditionally dealt. In the past, aircraft had always been ordered in small batches, denying manufacturers the opportunity to draw up long-term production plans, or order materials or components in the sort of quantities that would reduce overheads and lower the price. Aircraft costs and numbers produced were considered state secrets, with members of Parliament often being loftily assured by defence ministers that discussion of such subjects was "not in the public interest".

The second aircraft was soon to be designated the Anglo-French Variable Geometry (AFVG). The UK and France had already been considering national VG designs, so the selection of such a configuration seemed sensible. France had been design leader on the Jaguar programme, working in collaboration with BAC, but for AFVG these roles were reversed – a factor which probably helped to scuttle the programme. To this day, France is not prepared to see its aerospace industry take anything but the leading role in collaborative military ventures. This single-minded determination has won France a major share of the export market in supersonic warplanes, but can be the kiss of death for multi-national programmes.

British interest in the use of variable geometry (VG) dates back to 1946, when Sir Barnes Wallis (designer of the the wartime Wellington bomber, the Tall-boy heavy bomb and other specialized weapons) wrote a paper which investi-gated tailless configurations with mov-

Above: Mirage G8.01 (two-seat) and 02 in flight with wings spread (leading edge angle 23°). With twin Atar 9K-50 engines in place of the original Mirage G's single TF30, the G8 was otherwise similar to the earlier aircraft, which itself drew heavily on AFVG studies.

Right: The only major item of hardware to emerge from the AFVG airframe programme was this Warton mock-up. The engine was used in non-afterburning form on the short-lived VFW-614 airliner. Although larger than Tornado, the AFVG used a similar configuration.

able wings. Trials with unmanned models in the Wild Goose programme between 1949 and 1954 tested the basic configuration, and were followed by trials from 1955 onward of Swallow unmanned models. A manned experimental aircraft known as the JC.9 was built in the 1950s by Heston Aircraft, but it was never flown.

By late 1958 this research was being partly funded by the US Mutual Weapons Project Office, but work on Swallow ended in 1959. In some circles the legend persists to this day that the US had somehow stolen the UK idea for eventual use in the F-111 programme, but this romantic view overlooks the fact that Swallow test flights seem to have ended because US wind-tunnel testing had shown that the design had serious

subsonic pitch-up problems and lacked the promised high supersonic lift/drag figures.

The Warton design team had looked at variable sweep back in 1958 when studying the TSR-2 requirement, and even built test rigs, but very little information was available on bearings able to take very heavy loads while being asked to make intermittent movements of less than 90°, and it was concluded that VG represented too great a risk, so the aircraft was designed and built with a fixed delta wing instead.

British and French VG projects
Britain had not lost interest in VG. The first UK "paper" applications of VG were probably the Vickers ER.206 design proposed to meet a joint Naval-Air Staff

Target 346 for a multi-role fighter for service in the 1970s. Other designs were to follow, but none was ever built.

The most significant of these stillborn VG types was proposed in 1963 when BAC Warton drew up plans for a small VG aircraft, the P.45, which could be used as an advanced trainer or a light strike aircraft, and later developed into an air-superiority fighter. The P.45 was much smaller than the F-111: powered by two Rolls-Royce RB.172 afterburning turbofans or a single afterburning Spey, it was roughly in the same weight class as the Mirage III. A brochure was published in May 1964, but the RAF's requirement for a supersonic trainer was eventually met by the Anglo/French Jaguar.

Although never built, the P.45 was to have a strong influence on the future development of European VG aircraft. The chosen configuration was different in many ways from that of the General Dynamics F-111 then taking shape at Fort Worth. The wing pivots were further inboard than those on the US design, the horizontal tail was set lower on the fuselage (correcting one of the most serious deficiencies of the F-111 configuration), and the ducts which led the air from the inlets to the engine were much longer than the problem-ridden short ducts on the F-111.

France had been conducting its own VG studies since 1960 and by 1964 was already designing the variable-geometry Mirage G, an aircraft close in size and performance to the proposed AFVG. France could not afford to fund two aircraft for the same role; officially at least, the AFVG was the chosen candidate of the pair.

A basic AFVG specification was agreed by Britain and France in the summer of 1965. The aircraft was to be able to meet the RAF and Armée de l'Air requirements for a long-range strike aircraft, while being small enough to operate from France's *Clemenceau* class aircraft carriers. The result was an aircraft slightly smaller and lighter than the US F-111, but broadly in the same per-

formance class. Featuring tandem seating, long intake ducts with Mirage III-style intakes and a low-set horizontal tailplane, it would have been powered by two all-new European SNECMA/Bristol M45G afterburning turbofans.

Dassault continued to work on the Mirage G as a private venture, and in October 1965 the company was given a development contract. France was probably never really convinced that the UK intended to buy the AFVG, given the recent British propensity to purchase US aircraft and the intention to purchase the F-111. If the RAF wanted an interim strike aircraft to serve until the AFVG was ready, Dassault was prepared to develop a Spey-engined version of the Mirage IV bomber. This could have been delivered in 1969 with French avionics, or the early 1970s if a more sophisticated British suite (perhaps based on TSR.2 systems) was wanted, but the UK rejected this design, determined to obtain the F-111.

Britain's F-111 option was due to run until December 31, 1965, but the Labour government – enmeshed in a lengthy process of "reviewing" (a word which sounded more positive than "cancelling") Britain's defence requirements – had to request a two-month extension. On February 22, 1966, the British government announced that an order would be placed for 50 F-111K fighter-bombers at an agreed ceiling price of $5.95 million.

By the beginning of 1968 the first two aircraft were almost complete, and another 17 were following on down the line. In 1965, the F-111K was, in the words of Prime Minister Harold Wilson, "a bargain", but by now he was clearly thinking again, and in January 1968, the RAF order was cancelled. No clear reason was given, but the technical problems being experienced with the USAF versions and the desire to reduce defence spending were probably the main factors in the decision.

The prototype Mirage G was rolled out on May 27, 1967, and on June 11, even before it had flown, French Defence Minister Pierre Messmer delivered the

Above: The now-familiar lines of the Tornado IDS took shape for the first time with the construction of this full-scale mock-up. The only major feature absent was the air inlet which was added subsequently at the base of the vertical stabilizer.

Below: The first MRCA prototype – still in an incomplete state – is towed out of the hangar at MBB. The move took place before dawn and in conditions of secrecy, and the first photograph was not released until the airframe was externally complete.

death-blow to the ailing AFVG project, announcing that France could not afford to fund the programme in 1968 and 1969 and was unlikely to be able to do so in the early 1970s.

Mirage breakthrough

Two days before Messmer's announcement M48 Patton tanks, under the command of General Israel Tal, rolled to a halt at the edges of the Suez Canal after a blitzkrieg which had driven the Egyptian Army out of Sinai. The opening blows in that campaign had been struck by Dassault warplanes in the shape of the IDFAF's Mirage IIICJ fighters. Following this spectacular success the ageing Marcel Dassault was elevated almost overnight to the aerospace equivalent of superstar status, and the Mirage III production line was soon to become virtually a licence to print money as friend and foe of Israel alike scrambled to place orders for the delta-winged warplane. French confidence in its aerospace prowess soared.

On June 29, 1967, Messmer met his British opposite number, Denis Healey, in London and confirmed France's intention to withdraw from the programme. AFVG was dead, and the UK would have to look elsewhere for its next fighter; accordingly, in October 1967 the British government awarded contracts to BAC Warton and Rolls-Royce (who had taken over Bristol Siddeley) for a six-month study of a strike-oriented aircraft derivative of the AFVG.

The Mirage G flew for the first time at Istres in November. Within a month it had fully swept its wings, and within two had exceeded Mach 2. It was eventually to be lost in an accident in January 1971, but only months later the twin-engined Mirage G8 was flying. This was a heavier VG aircraft powered by two afterburning Atars and fitted with a Cyrano IV radar and a nav/attack system based on that of the Jaguar.

The Mirage G8 was never to see operational service. Like the even more ambitious Mirage G4, a proposed predecessor to the G8 which would have been powered by two of SNECMA's new M53 afterburning turbofans, it proved too expensive for a defence budget already stretched by IRBM and SLBM strategic missile programmes. Faced with the need to equip the Armée de l'Air with less expensive aircraft, France abandoned VG and turned to lighter single-seat, single-engined designs, developing the Mirage F1 and 2000.

Above: BAC chief test pilot Paul Millet takes D-9591, the first prototype (P.01), on its maiden flight on August 14, 1974. Fifteen days later MBB's Nils Meister took the aircraft to supersonic speed for the first time during the third sortie, also from Manching.

Below: Flight tests with P.01 soon showed that the aircraft would be a stable and comfortable mount when flying at the low levels needed to ensure survival during the strike missions into heavily defended airspace for which it was designed.

Above: Repainted in a camouflage finish, XX946 refuels from a Handley Page Victor tanker. Flight refuelling was given high priority, since the technique would allow trials aircraft to stay airborne longer, maximizing the amount of data which could be gathered on a single sortie.

Right: Another task assigned to XX946 was flutter testing with external stores. On this sortie the aircraft carried tanks and ECM pods on the wing pylons, the pods being aerodynamic dummies to simulate the operational RAF fit of Sky Shadow (port) and BOZ 107 (starboard).

Below: The first prototype to have fully-variable inlets was P.02 (XX946), the first Warton-built aircraft. Able to reach higher speeds than its predecessor, it quickly expanded the performance envelope.

Starfighter replacement

Britain was not the only nation shopping for a new fighter during the late 1960s. Under a massive international programme started in 1959-60, West Germany, Italy, Belgium, Denmark, Norway and the Netherlands had built the F-104G Starfighter under licence from Lockheed. By 1968 European production was virtually complete, although Italy was to press on into the mid-1970s with production of the specialized F-104S interceptor. This massive F-104G fleet would need to be replaced in the middle to late 1970s, as would other supersonic fighters such as the Canadian and Dutch F-5A/B fleets and, on a slightly later timescale, Belgium's Mirage 5s.

The US aerospace industry not surprisingly wanted this prize to fall into its hands, and in the mid-1960s Northrop began the task of developing an agile fighter intended to replace the F-5 series. Possible users of a new fighter included existing NATO operators of the F-104 – Belgium, Canada, Italy, the Netherlands and West Germany – while Australia had an obvious requirement for a Mirage replacement. By 1967 the company had concluded that a good market

existed for a Mach 2 air-superiority fighter with good secondary interdiction and close-support capabilities – a fighter able to combat and defeat whatever the Mikoyan bureau might field as an eventual replacement for the MiG-21.

Almost a decade of market studies and project-definition work resulted in the P-530 Cobra, ancestor of the present-day F/A-18 Hornet. This eventually embodied the result of more than 4,000 hours of wind-tunnel testing using 15 models, but despite all its efforts, Northrop never did persuade anyone to order the P-530.

A Cobra mock-up was built in 1970, and details of the configuration were publicly released in 1971. By 1972 the company had invested $22 million of private-venture money in the P-530, but it understandably baulked at the estimated cost of building and flying two prototypes – around $100 million at early 1970s prices. Ironically for Northrop, the new design was later to play a minor role in helping to get the Tornado programme under way.

Northrop was not the only company with its eye on the NATO market: Lockheed was drawing up plans for its own

Starfighter replacement. The CL-1200 Lancer was a high-wing design based on the F-104 and using many common structural components and systems, but powered by a single TF30 engine. By 1969 this had been revised to create the further improved CL-1200-2, but there were no takers.

Bizarre proposal

One US proposal which had attracted German interest during the mid-1960s was the collaborative Advanced Vertical Strike (AVS) fighter. One of the most bizarre designs ever proposed for service use, this was being tackled by Fairchild and EWR-Sud (a consortium consisting of Messerschmitt, Bölkow, and Heinkel). In basic configuration it resembled a slimmer version of the F-111, with tandem seating for the crew and the air inlets mounted side by side above the wing centre section, while to provide VTOL capability it used a propulsion system similar to that later adopted for the Yakovlev Yak-38 'Forger'. The jet pipes of the General Electric main propulsion engines could be vectored downward, while no fewer than four Rolls-Royce/Allison XJ99 lift jets were located just behind the cockpit and immediately beneath the wing glove. Doors on either side of the fuselage opened, allowing the lift jets to be swung out clear of the wing glove.

AVS concept-definition studies were completed in 1967, but the high cost of a six-year project-definition phase and the construction of prototype hardware caused the project to be abandoned. By the year before, the writing had been clearly on the wall for AVS, so at the beginning of 1967 Germany began studies of a small single-seat VG aircraft known as Neue Kampfflugzeug (NKF). Work on AVS gradually ended.

On July 10, 1967, less than a month after France's torpedoing of the AFVG, a BAC team visited EWR-Sud to discuss possible collaboration, particularly in the field of VG. The Italian government also showed interest in possible collaboration, and formal negotiations between the UK and West Germany began later that month.

A brochure on the proposed UKVG aircraft was issued on November 30. This aircraft was not at all what the Luftwaffe had in mind. Being derived from the AFVG, it remained a large long-range aircraft in the F-111 performance class. SNECMA had abandoned the M45G, so the UKVG had been forced to investigate UK solutions, first the BS.143 and BS.145 turbofans, then the RB.153. The last was an afterburning turbofan developed jointly by Rolls-Royce and MAN-Turbomotoren and run for the first time in November 1963. These UKVG proposals were backed up by a limited amount of hardware, with BAC having started work late in 1967 on an experimental wing pivot and wing box.

In addition to requiring an F-104 replacement, Germany also had the problem of replacing the Fiat G.91. The British proposed that the Luftwaffe should adopt Jaguar as a G.91 replacement and join in the manufacturing programme, then join with the UK on a VG programme based on UKVG or the P.45, but the Jaguar deal never got off the ground, Northrop's P-530 Cobra studies having convinced the Germans that a single type could meet all Germany's requirements. Further discussions held with the UK in December confirmed that the two nations still had very different ideas on the size of a next-generation fighter, and that Germany's relatively inexperienced aircraft industry would be reluctant to enter into an AFVG-style agreement giving the UK design leadership of the programme.

The German government realised that it would be difficult on cost grounds to develop the NKF as an all-German project, so the decision was taken to invite other NATO nations to join in a collaborative effort, and in January 1968 the main users of the F-104G – Germany, Italy, Belgium and the Netherlands – drew up a joint requirement for a Starfighter replacement, proposing a small single-seat STOL aircraft with the designation Multi-Role Aircraft for 1975 (MRA-75). Although also an F-104 user, Canada was at that time studying its own Canadian Multi-Role Aircraft (CAMRA) project, but took observer status on MRA-75.

While this was going on the British government was once again reviewing its defence posture, concluding early in 1968 that its main military role lay in Europe and that its equipment should be designed with this in mind. BAC was accordingly ordered to revise the UKVG into a shorter-range design, the resulting Advanced Combat Aircraft (ACA) being similar in weight to NKF.

Despite this, the UK did not participate in early MRA-75 discussions. Britain was studying a twin BS.143-powered Future Combat Aircraft able to meet UK and German strike requirements, and also the interceptor requirements of the other MRA-75 partners. This design was slightly larger than that proposed for NKF, an was offered as a solution to the MRA-75 requirements.

Each of the nations involved had its own idea of what type of fighter it wanted. The RAF needed a two-seat strike aircraft with all-weather nav/attack systems, for example, while Germany wanted a level of STOL capability which would allow MRA-75 to operate from war-damaged airstrips; Canada and the Netherlands demanded that the aircraft have the high Specific Excess Power (SEP) needed to match their interceptor requirements; and Italy also wanted an interceptor.

Faced with requirements for aircraft able to replace both the F-104G and G.91, and the evidence from Northrop's P-530 Cobra design that a single type could meet its close-support, strike, reconnaissance and air-superiority needs,

Germany still found the concept of procuring only one new fighter attractive. But this involved one compromise: such a multi-role warplane would be closer in size to the UK's FCA than to Germany's NKF. That compromise was deemed acceptable, and the notion of a slightly heavier aircraft cleared the way for a collaborative venture.

With German and British now thinking along similar lines, events moved quickly, and on July 25, 1968, Britain, West Germany, Belgium, Canada, Italy and the Netherlands signed an MoU expressing their interest in the proposed new fighter. Britain, Canada, Germany and the Netherlands all agreed to fund feasibility studies.

The air arms of the partners had all contributed to an Operational Equipment Objective (OEO) which laid down the desired performance. Two of these parameters, mission weight and SEP, were of crucial importance, since they had a strong influence on the size and weight of the eventual design. Canadian and Dutch demands for the high SEP needed by their interceptor missions increased the size of the wing and the thrust of the engines, for example, while these factors in turn demanded that more fuel be carried to maintain the range demanded by potential users such as the UK. BAC, MBB and Canadair all tried their hand at creating a suitable design, producing the results in August.

By the end of the year, Canada and Belgium had dropped out of the programme. Belgium had never been a very staunch supporter of the project,

and its industry was already busy, having been given a significant share of the Mirage 5 manufacturing task. Canada had begun a re-think of its limited defence commitments, and had decided that it had no near-term requirement for an MRCA-type aircraft.

The next task was to fix the size and weight of the aircraft, a process which involved attempting to create a realistic requirement shorn of some of the more extreme demands which had been cranked into the OEO document. By mid-December 1968 the Joint Industrial Company (JIC) formed by representatives of BAC, MBB and Fiat had drawn up what they saw as a reasonable requirement which would result in an aircraft which would be both combat-effective and affordable.

Rival designs

By the end of December two rival designs existed. Like the three created several months earlier, each had twin engines, a VG wing and a single vertical tail. The BAC submission was perhaps the more conventional looking, a high-wing design showing the influence of the earlier AFVG and UKVG designs with the wing pivot located within the fuselage. The MBB design had a mid-position wing and lines which vaguely resembled those of the single-tail configuration originally proposed for the Grumman F-14 Tomcat. In this case the wing pivot was located well outboard of the fuselage.

The result worked out in the first few months of 1969 was a compromise reached not by a simple trade-off, but by the British and German design teams appreciating the good points of each other's submissions. The wing glove on the MBB design gave better manoeuvrability, for example, while BAC's high wing allowed engines to be removed by dropping them out of the fuselage, a technique which required less free space than pulling the engine out via the rear of the aircraft.

On March 14, 1969, a technical meeting held at Munich agreed a mutually acceptable configuration with a high wing incorporating outboard pivots and a wing glove. This baseline configuration was officially published, and twelve days later (March 26) the Panavia industrial consortium was formed to handle development of the aircraft.

BAC and MBB each had a one-third share, while Fiat and Fokker-VFW had one-sixth shares, and under the original scheme five aircraft plants were in-

Left: XX947, the second prototype built by Warton and the third example to fly, was the first Tornado to have dual controls. In the configuration shown here it carried eight 1,000lb (450kg) bombs, two 330Imp gal (1,500lit) tanks and two ECM pods.

Below: One potentially hazardous task assigned to XX947 was stall and spin trials. To reduce the risk, the aircraft was fitted with a tail-mounted spin recovery parachute plus an emergency power unit able to restart both engines if necessary.

volved. Britain, Germany and Italy would each have their own assembly line, building aircraft from major sub-assemblies created by the other partners in the programme.

The aircraft was by now known as the Multi-Role Combat Aircraft (MRCA), and two versions were planned – a single-seat version which would meet the German, Italian and Dutch interceptor requirements, and a two-seater suitable for the British and German Navy interdiction strike role. Most of the structure and systems of the two versions would be identical, but the two-seater would have wings with integral fuel tanks in order to meet the RAF's greater range requirements. The avionics would vary to meet the individual national requirements, with the two-seater carrying a more complex suite than any of the single-seaters. The single-seat project would be led by MBB at Munich, the two-seater by BAC at Warton. The two configurations were often referred to by the designations Panavia 100 and Panavia 200 respectively.

BAC's Warton division would develop and build the rear fuselage of the aircraft, plus the front fuselage of the two-seat version, and run the UK assembly line. MBB's Military Aircraft Group at Manching, 50 miles (80km) north of Munich, would tackle the fuselage centre section including the wing box and pivots, and be responsible for the German assembly line, leaving VFW to build the front fuselage of the single-seat aircraft. Aeritalia's Combat Aircraft Group at Casalle, 10 miles (16km) north of Turin, would be responsible for the wings and for the Italian assembly line, while Fokker built the tail surfaces.

A joint governmental NATO MRCA Management Organisation, known as NAMMO, was set up to act as the official customer for the planned multi-national fighter, and consisted of the senior government and military personnel involved with running the programme. This in turn had an executive branch known as NAMMA (NATO MRCA Management Agency), which was set up to manage the project in conformity with NATO rules and regulations. Two months later the UK West Germany and Italy formally committed themselves to the definition phase of the project.

In July 1969 the Netherlands announced that it was withdrawing from the programme, claiming that the MRCA would be too complex and expensive and that it would not be available until "well after 1975" – too late to meet the RNethAF's requirements. With the departure of Fokker-VFW from the programme, BAC became responsible for all front fuselage sections and for the tail surfaces. Shares in Panavia were redistributed as follows: BAC 42.5 per cent, MBB 42.5 per cent and Fiat 15 per cent.

The next problem was to choose a suitable powerplant. The story of engine development and selection is recounted in detail later in this book. For the moment it is sufficient to note that Pratt & Whitney, General Electric and Rolls-Royce all offered afterburning turbofan engines, but the successful contender was the three-shaft Rolls-Royce RB.199. Following the selection of this engine in September 1969 the Turbo-Union international consortium was established to handle engine development and manufacture.

The avionics carried by MRCA would obviously be much more complex than those fitted to any previous NATO tactical aircraft, so a tri-national consortium known as Avionics System Engineering was set up on September 26, 1969. Jointly owned by EASAMS (UK), ESG (Germany) and SIA (Italy), this proved unworkable, and the job was later passed to EASAMS, which in turn placed work-sharing sub-contracts with ESG and SIA.

The outside world had its first alleged view of the aircraft in September 1969 with the display of a model which purported to show the Panavia 100 single-seat version of the aircraft. It was so inaccurate as to verge on the absurd. The wing pivots were shown in the AFVG-style inboard location which had been abandoned six months earlier, the tiny size of the canopy suggested a massive aircraft of F-111 proportions, while the fuselage sides sported a magnificent pair of "Flight Falsies".

"Flight Falsies"

For the benefit of readers unfamiliar with this term of aeronautical abuse, it was coined in 1956 by the British aviation journal *Flight International* to describe the hemispherical metal fairings used to conceal the then-secret intakes of the Lockheed F-104A during the roll-out ceremony of the first example. Beneath these covers were the then-new semicircular intakes with half-cone centrebodies, a highly successful concept used to this day by the Mirage series. In the case of MRCA, the demands of "security" had apparently caused the ten-year-old concept of "Flight Falsies" to be revived, and the model on show had no air intakes – the fuselage sides simply blended into the nose section.

The purpose served by faking on such a blatant scale is hard to fathom. When the MRCA intakes were finally unveiled, the rest of the aviation world – and the intelligence community – must have derived some amusement from the fact that the type of intake used on Tornado was not a new configuration, but a well-established design similar to that flying

Above right: D-9592 (P.04), first flown at Manching on September 2, 1975, was the first prototype to have the integrated avionic system and was used during the subsequent flight test programme to demonstrate automatic terrain following.

Right: X-586 (P.05) was the first Italian-built prototype, flying for the first time on December 5, 1975. Assigned to flutter testing, it crashed on the sixth flight, but after a two-year rebuild it was restored to flying status and rejoined the trials programme.

on the North American A-5 Vigilante since 1958 and on the MiG-25 'Foxbat' since the early 1960s.

Project definition work was completed in April 1970, three months then being lost before the various governments finally ordered pre-development to begin. Another important goal was achieved in September 1971, when the RB.199 engine began running on the bench. Within a year and a half it was flying in a Vulcan bomber testbed. Having completed a review of the programme, on March 15, 1973, the three governments authorized Panavia to begin preparations for production, a process which involved manufacturing the necessary tooling and the ordering of long-lead items and raw materials.

By this time, the number of aircraft required could be accurately determined. The original plans had involved more than 1,000, Germany being the largest customer with a stated (but hopelessly optimistic) requirement for around 700. The departure of the Canadians and Dutch, plus cutbacks in the German requirement to around 420 then finally to 324, reduced the planned production run to 809 aircraft.

The need for a two-seat operational trainer version resulted in the original fuselage length being extended by around 20in (50cm). This stretch, plus the growing realization by the Luftwaffe that the simple avionics suite being proposed for its single-seat aircraft might not be effective in the 1980s and beyond, led the service to switch its purchase to the RAF-style two-seater. Although the Italian Air Force had never operated a two-seat fighter, it accepted the German decision and agreed to switch its purchase to two-seaters, and the single-seat version was duly abandoned.

The programme involved nine prototypes: the UK was responsible for assembling four, while three would be built in West Germany and two in Italy. These would be followed by six pre-production aircraft, three British, two German and one Italian.

To extract the maximum amount of information from each flying hour Panavia decided that the prototypes would be fitted with telemetry equipment able to transmit over a radio link data from up to 460 instrumented points on the aircraft and its systems. Ground equipment able simultaneously to monitor and record up to 150 parameters was installed at each of the three flight-test centres. This also provided a voice communications link between the aircrew, the test controller and several engineers, who were able to monitor the flight via real-time data displayed on CRT screens, pen recorders and conventional dial instruments.

First prototype

The first prototype, registered D-9591, was completed in the autumn of 1973, and was shipped from Ottobrunn to Manching on November 12, where it was due to carry out taxiing trials using engines cleared for ground running only, then receive flight-rated RB.199s in time to make its first flight early in 1974. This schedule proved hopelessly optimistic, partly due to delays in clearing the RB.199 for flight. The aircraft was not to fly until August 14. Pilot for the first sortie was Paul Millet, then BAC's chief test pilot and project pilot for the MRCA programme, with MBB's Nils Meister in the rear seat.

For this first mission the aircraft was lightly loaded to a take-off weight of around 39,000lb (17,690kg), only about two-thirds of the maximum take-off weight planned for the operational fighter. Taking off with partial flap, wings fully forward and maximum afterburner, the prototype climbed away at a steepening angle in order to avoid exceeding the gear-down airspeed limits.

Above: XX948 was the sixth prototype. Built at Warton and flown for the first time on December 30, 1975, it was the first to carry the internally mounted 27mm cannon. This photograph shows the guns being test-fired at altitude during a sortie flown in June 1981.

Escorted by two chase planes – a TF-104G and a G.91T – D-9591 climbed to a cruising height of 10,000ft (3,000m), where Millet was able to fly a simulated approach in order to check out the landing procedure. Having raised the undercarriage and retracted the flaps, Millet was then able to assess handling at speeds of up to 300kt before returning to Manching for landing. Two approaches were flown – a pre-planned missed approach, then a landing made at around 20kt faster than the touchdown speed which would be used later in the programme. Total flight time was around 30 minutes: Millet and Meister achieved all the goals planned for the maiden flight, and reported no system failures or spurious fault indications.

Following several days of planned work on the aircraft, bad weather delayed a resumption of flying. The second sortie was finally flown on August 21, and saw the wings moved in flight for the first time (one flight ahead of schedule) and set to an intermediate angle of 45°. The effect of the airbrakes was explored, and the aircraft was flown through simulated single-engine approach and overshoot patterns. Other tests checked the effects on handling of some failure modes.

For the third flight, on August 29, the crew had sufficient confidence to change places – a move not planned until sortie 4. Meister swept the wings back to 68° and took the aircraft supersonic for the first time, reaching a maximum speed of Mach 1.15.

Below: 98+06 (P.07), first flown on March 30, 1976, the second avionics trials aircraft, leads a formation of the first three prototypes to be assembled in Germany. D-9592 (top) carries a camera pod under the fuselage to record the trials in progress.

Above: A Kormoran ignites its rocket motor after release from X-587 (P.09), the first pre-series aircraft. This was the first firing of the MBB anti-ship missile from Tornado and took place at the Sardinia missile range on July 31, 1978.

D-9591 was to have a long career, and in later life would be re-registered 98+04. Being the first prototype, it was soon unrepresentative of the definitive and evolving configuration, so could not be used for tasks such as measuring drag and performance. Assigned to engine-test duties, it was used in 1978 to test-fly the more powerful -04 engines, and by 1980 was being used for production engine assessment.

The second prototype, XX946, the first British aircraft, flew at Warton on October 30 of the same year. Unlike the German aircraft, this had fully-variable engine inlets, allowing it to be flown at high speed. Its initial task was flight envelope expansion and engine development, but an early priority for 1975 flight testing was to carry out preliminary flight-refuelling trials. Once the technique was proven, the use of flight-refuelling would allow sortie time to be increased, maximizing the amount of data which could be obtained from a single mission. First tests were carried out in conjunction with a Handley Page Victor tanker of the RAF

The following year, 1975, saw four more aircraft join the fleet. XX947, flown at Warton on August 5, was the first dual-control aircraft, and one task assigned to this third prototype was that of stall and spin behaviour. To make these tests as safe as possible the aircraft was fitted with a tail-mounted spin-recovery parachute, plus a Sunstrand emergency power unit designed to cope with the possibility of a double flameout.

Right: X-587 in semi-operational colour scheme carrying eight BL 755 cluster bombs; wing pylons mount Sidewinders (inner) and dummy ECM pods (outer), but no tanks are fitted.

Powered by a hydrazine monopropellant, it could generate sufficient power to allow the engines to be relit. One surprising feature of the operational aircraft is that such a unit is not fitted as standard. The logic may well have been that the crew of a low-flying aircraft which loses both engines have no time for a re-light.

D-9592 (later 98+05), which flew from Manching on September 2, was the first to be fitted with integrated avionic system. This aircraft played a vital part in clearing Tornado for production, being tasked with proving the avionics and demonstrating automatic flight at low level. By 1977 it was being used for weapons trials, including flight-testing of the sideways-firing MW-1 submunitions dispenser, but its primary function was to be avionics testing. By 1980 it was involved in trials of the digital autopilot, navigation and radar ground-mapping.

Flutter trials

First Italian prototype was X-586, flown at Casalle on December 5 and assigned to flutter testing. In January of the following year it made a heavy landing at Casalle at the end of the sixth flight of its brief career. Over-sensitivity in the pitch channel of the CSAS caused the nose to hit the ground so heavily that extensive damage ensued. Flutter trials were re-assigned to the second prototype, while X-586 went back into the Casalle works for a major rebuild involving the replacement of the forward fuselage. Just over two years later, the aircraft returned to flight status.

Given the lack of fully-rated engines, Tornado was restricted in speed and height for the first few years of test flying: when the magazine *Air International* reported on flight-test progress in the late summer of 1976 maximum speed was around Mach 1.3, and the aircraft had reached some 40,000ft (12,000m).

Early test flights showed signs of directional instability at transonic speed. Between Mach 0.9 and 0.95 stability was reduced to an unacceptably low value, and wool-tufting the rear fuselage revealed that the flow of air around the rear spine and the base of the vertical fin was

breaking away, reducing fin effectiveness. This proved tricky to cure, with more than 20 revised configurations of the area being tested before an acceptable solution was devised, the answer being to slim the lines of the rear fuselage and add a longer fairing under the vertical fin.

Directional instability was also noted when using maximum reverse thrust after landing. The third prototype was to skid off the Warton runway on October 4, 1976, during a landing in heavy rain, losing its main undercarriage in the process. (The crew were unhurt, and their mount was duly repaired and returned to trials duty). In this case, the engine efflux from the thrust reversers was found to be disturbing the airflow around the fin; the solution adopted was to use yaw rate data from the CSAS to control nosewheel steering.

The rear-fuselage restyling dictated by the airflow breakaway problem resulted in a distinct change in the external shape of Tornado, seen for the first time on the last prototype flown in 1975.

Below: Like the production programme, the task of building prototype and pre-production aircraft was split between Britain, West Germany and Italy. This is X-587, the first pre-series aircraft and the second Italian-built Tornado.

Warton's XX948, which made its maiden flight on December 20, was the sixth prototype, the first with the new slimmer rear fuselage, and the first to carry the internal gun. The following year, this aircraft carried out the first release of external stores.

Seventh prototype and first to carry a near-complete avionics suite, was 98+06, flown at Manching on March 30 of the following year and soon involved in terrain-following and other avionics trials, sharing these duties with 98+04 (the redesignated fourth prototype).

The three nations now decided to commit the aircraft to production, signing a memorandum to this effect in June 1976. Production was formally authorized with the placing of an order for the first

batch of 40 aircraft on July 29, 1976, two weeks after the flight of XX950 – the Warton-built eighth prototype – on July 15. This aircraft was assigned to avionics development and weapon aiming tests.

By this time, the interdiction/strike (IDS) version of Tornado had been joined by a second model known as the Air Defence Variant. A specialized interceptor intended to serve only with the Royal Air Force, this aircraft was ordered into full-scale development on March 4, 1976; the subsequent development of this version will be recounted later in this chapter.

Pre-series examples of the basic IDS version began flying in 1977. The first two flew on the same day, February 5, 1977, and were the ninth and 11th aircraft

respectively (No. 10, a static-test airframe, was never flown) in the growing fleet. No. 9 was X-587, flown at Casalle, while the 11th was Manching's 98+01, a dual-control aircraft.

X-587 started life tasked with flutter tests, and trials with external stores and weapons. The second half of 1979 was to see it based at Decimomannu air base in Sardinia for armament, autopilot and climatic tests, while in 1980 it was used for trials of the MBB Kormoran anti-ship missile.

On earlier aircraft the rear end of the fairing beneath the vertical fin had terminated just aft of the rudder hinge, but the revised design first flown on 98+01 extends to the rudder trailing edge. The flight testing needed to confirm the

success of this final tail-area fix delayed its delivery to the German Official Test Centre at Manching until early 1980.

Three Official Test Centres (OTCs) were set up, one at Manching, one at Boscombe Down in England, and the third at Pratica di Mare, Italy. First aircraft to be delivered to one of these units was the 12th Tornado, XZ630: flown at Warton on March 14, 1977, it was ferried to the A&AEE at Boscombe Down on February 3, 1978.

The final four pre-series aircraft came ever-closer to the production configuration. Janaury 10, 1978, saw the flight at Manching of the 13th Tornado, and the first to have the definitive pattern of tailerons. These have a kinked leading edge designed to ensure that aeroelastic deflection of the wing and taileron cannot result in mutual interference when the wings are fully swept.

Delays with the 14th aircraft resulted in the 15th being the next to fly. Built by Warton, XZ631 was the first to have the production-standard rear fuselage and "wet" fin, and was flown on November 24, 1978. The 14th aircraft made it into the air at Casalle on January 9, 1979. X-588 was the first aircraft to have production-standard wings. The production-standard forward fuselage was first incorporated in the final pre-series aircraft, 98+03, flown at Manching on March 26.

Even as the final pre-series aircraft were being delivered, production aircraft were moving down the assembly lines. The first to be rolled out were dual-control trainers. The roll-out ceremony for BT.001 (ZA319) at Warton on June 5, 1979, was followed a day later by the roll-out of GT.001 (43+01) at Manching. These aircraft flew on July 10 and 20 respectively. At this time, a third batch of 110 aircraft was ordered, bringing the total number under contract to 314.

First UK production example of the strike configuration was BS.001, flown for the first time late in the afternoon of March 14, 1980, at Warton, with deputy

Above: Warton's XZ631 (P.15) was the first pre-series aircraft to have a production-standard rear fuselage and the 'wet' pattern of tail fin. Officially designated the 15th Tornado, it beat the Italian-built 14th example into the air by six weeks.

Below: German Tornado 43+63 lands at a mist-shrouded RAF Cottesmore, home of the Trinational Tornado Training Establishment (TTTE), in February 1981, six months after the first examples had arrived at the base.

Right: 98+03 (P.16), in Marineflieger colours and wearing the fin flash of Erprobungsstelle (service trials unit) 61, carries out a submunitions ejection demonstration with the MBB MW-1 dispenser, a standard weapon for Luftwaffe Tornados.

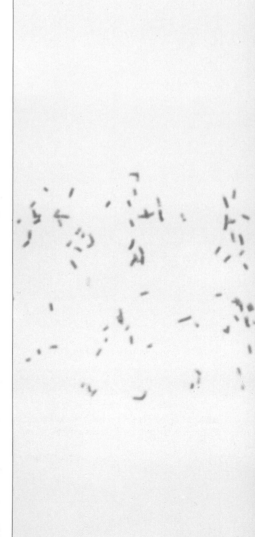

Right: First production Tornado was ZA319, a Warton-built dual-control trainer, seen here on its first flight. It was officially rolled out on June 5, 1979, one day ahead of GT.001, the first German production trainer.

chief test pilot Jerry Lee in the front cockpit and chief navigator Ray Woollett in the back seat. During an initial 105-minute sortie the aircraft was taken up to supersonic speed. In July 1980 delivery of production aircraft to the Trinational Tornado Training Establishment (TTTE) was begun, and Tornado began its service career.

ADV for the RAF

The story of the RAF's Tornado Air Defence Variant is simpler to relate. In 1971 the Royal Air Force issued Air Staff Target 395, a requirement for a long-range interceptor able to replace the Phantom and Lightning. At a time when the US services tended to view the Soviet MiG-25 'Foxbat' as a major threat, and the USAF was drawing up a requirement for highly agile fighters, the RAF took a more traditional view, asking for a long-range interceptor able to patrol 500nm or more north of the UK.

The threat the new interceptor would face was not next-generation agile Soviet fighters – these relatively short-range aircraft would be dealt with by the air forces of other NATO Allies located closer to the Warsaw Pact's main operating bases. Instead, the new fighter would need to deal with large formations of long-range strike aircraft and bombers operating at low level, attacking under the cover of bad weather or darkness and screened by the most sophisticated and intense jamming that the Soviet electronics industry could devise in the 1980s and 1990s.

Despite the adage that it is easier to convert a fighter into a strike aircraft than vice versa, the Panavia Tornado interdictor/strike aircraft displayed many of the performance parameters needed for a new interceptor: the level of air-to-air performance specified by the original requirements from Canada and the Netherlands had raised the performance above that required for the basic strike role, particularly in areas such as acceleration, climbing performance and specific excess power.

Neither of the other Panavia partners wanted a dedicated Tornado interceptor, so it was clear from an early stage that this would be a national project, with the UK having to foot the R&D bill for this new version.

As with the basic IDS version, components for the ADV are built by all three partners – Aeritalia (wings); British Aerospace Warton Division (front and rear fuselage, fin, and tail); and Messerschmitt-Bölkow-Blohm (centre fuselage and wing carry-through box) – with final assembly and flight test carried out at BAe Warton. Despite the changes described earlier, the aircraft still has around 80 per cent commonality with the original IDS version.

Full-scale development of Tornado ADV, formally launched on March 4, 1976, soon found itself the centre of controversy. With new Soviet strike aircraft such as the Sukhoi Su-24 'Fencer' and Tupolev Tu-22M 'Backfire' entering service in significant numbers, the British government found itself facing growing criticism over the depleted state of the UK's air defences. Calls were heard for the new fighter to be supplemented or even replaced by an off-the-shelf purchase of US fighters.

To have ignored the merits of the latest generation of US fighters would have been foolish, and the UK Ministry of Defence had in fact carried out studies of all three. The most promising was the Grumman F-14 Tomcat, but the radar and engines of this impressive US Navy interceptor reflected an earlier generation of technology, having been devised for the cancelled F-111B naval fighter. The McDonnell Douglas F-15, being a dedicated dogfighter, offered flight performance that was second to none, but studies showed that its single-seat cockpit and existing radar would not be able to meet the requirements of all-weather combat in the face of intense and sophisticated ECM: any RAF Eagle would require a new radar and a two-place cockpit. (Within a decade of this study,

Tornado production schedule				
Batch	IDS	ADV	Total	Delivery
4	144	18	162	Feb 84–Oct 85
5	119	52	171	May 85–Jun 87
6	63	92	155	Jun 87–Jul 89

the USAF was in fact to order a two-seat F-15E with an improved radar.) The smaller General Dynamics F-16 Fighting Falcon was never a serious contender.

The RAF wanted the ADV, said the UK MoD, and that was what they would get. Free from the threat posed by alternative aircraft, BAe and its Panavia partners were able to continue work on the new fighter, which would be known initially as Tornado F.2 in RAF service, and a batch of three prototypes were ordered to be built as quickly as possible.

Current production rate for Tornado is around 110 aircraft per year – approximately 42 each from the UK and West German assembly lines, plus 24 from the Italian line. The prototypes were built as part of batch 1, but production examples are being built as part of the later batches 4, 5 and 6.

First of the three prototypes was rolled out on August 9, 1979, and flown for the first time on October 27 of that year; all three ADV prototypes were flying within 13 months. A01, tasked with handling and performance trials, was the first to be fitted with the Spin Prevention and Incidence Limiting System (SPILS). A02 was the weapon system and avionics development aircraft; initially used for Sky Flash missile trials, it was later used to test the Mauser cannon. A03, the first to be fitted with the AI24 radar, has been used for radar and weapon system integration work.

The first two production Tornado F.2s were officially rolled out in late March 1984, though the occasion was strictly ceremonial; the first had already flown on March 5. These aircraft were sent to A&AEE Boscombe Down before being delivered to the RAF.

Media controversy

Throughout its development, Tornado was to be the subject of frequent political and media attacks. At times, "Tornado knocking" showed signs of becoming one of the few growth industries of the mid-1970s, as pundits solemnly denounced it as being too expensive, too complex, and too low in performance. Preparing his own book, *Panavia Tornado*, back in the late 1970s, Bill Gunston noted that, in the UK alone, "at least four major TV programmes, 10 radio feature broadcasts, and 270 newspaper articles" had attacked the programme.

He probably included the present author among the anti-Tornado faction, commenting unfavourably on my 1979 suggestion in the pages of *Flight International* that the McDonnell Douglas F/A-18 might be a better buy for many customers. (Despite my enthusiasm for

Tornado, I remain unrepentant. For a nation wishing to deploy only one model of fighter for multi-role service, I would still back the McDonnell Douglas warplane. The Australian, Canadian and Spanish Air Forces seem to have agreed with me.)

Tornado performance is a subject for a later chapter, but the general question of performance deficiencies may be swiftly dispatched with the observation that Tornado aircrew were conspicuously absent from the ranks of the knockers. Prototype and pre-series IDS aircraft were distinctly lacking in thrust, but the early Mk 101 powerplant has now given way to the more powerful Mk 103 to remedy that deficiency.

The cost question is a thornier one. The concept that modern fighters are over-expensive reflects the values of an earlier era, and largely ignores the massive inflation of the last 15 years. A nostalgic trip back to the heady days of the early 1970s is needed to set the scene in perspective – a world where the pound sterling was worth $2.40, the Israelis manned the Bar Lev line along the banks of the Suez Canal, the Arab "oil weapon" had yet to be used against the West, and the world economic recession was yet to come.

Back in those inexpensive days, Northrop was near the end of its F-5A programme, having cranked these supersonic lightweight fighters out of the door at a unit cost only $750,000, while Dassault could still deliver a Mirage III for around $1.8-1.9 million. Worried aircraft salesmen even forsaw the possibility that McDonnell Douglas might flood the market with a cheap single-seat derivative of the Phantom at a unit cost of less than $2.4 million.

Discussing fighter costs in that year, British aviation writer Roy Braybrook described how a Grumman representative had expressed the view that nobody could build an air superiority fighter at a cost of less than $10 million (£4.2 million at the exchange rate of the time). "This may be true in American terms," wrote Braybrook, "but someone will have to defend the skies of Europe for a lot less than that!"

Although the new F-5-21 (later designated F-5E) taking shape at Northrop was being offered at around $1.3 million, the next generation of US fighters had already cracked the $10 million barrier. The USAF's new F-15 Eagle was not due to fly for another year, but was already priced at $12 million a copy, while the US Navy had just flown its second F-14 prototype and was talking of a unit cost of $11.5 million.

At these prices, Tornado promised to be a bargain, the unit cost of the IDS version being anticipated at around $4.0 million. A year later, the USAF was to set a unit cost at 1972 prices of $3 million for production aircraft when requesting bids for the construction of prototypes of the proposed Lightweight Fighter, an aircraft whose strike capabilities fell far below those of the Panavia fighter.

These figures may seem like a long-lost Golden Age but general costs and salaries back in 1971 were a fraction of their current value. Your author had just been tempted away from employment at Hawker Siddeley Dynamics by a salary of £1,750, while best-selling author Len Deighton's novel *Bomber* has just appeared in paperback at a cost of 50p. Readers who possess a copy of Deighton's book can get their own clue to the effects of inflation by noting the date and cost of their edition. A lunchtime stroll to my local bookshop showed that the 1985 price of a paperback edition of *Bomber* is now £1.95. Typical cost of a new paperback best-seller is £2.95.

Using the cost of paperback books as a yardstick, inflation has pushed the cost of a best-seller up by a factor of around six. If fifteen years of inflation had pushed the cost of a military aircraft up by this amount, an F-5E would cost $7.8 million, and F-16 would be $18.0 million, Tornado IDS would carry a $24.0 million price tag, while the F-15 would be somewhere around $60.0 million! Luckily for the taxpayer, the price increases faced by air arms have been rather more modest than those faced by book buyers.

Preparing a list of comparative fighter costs is difficult. Methods of estimating costs can vary, while some manufacturers simply do not release figures. In the case of US aircraft, several fighters are available for each type, but the table below assumes FY85 flyaway price, while for non-US types estimates have been drawn from various industry and commercial sources. The dollar costs for Tornado were derived by assuming an exchange rate of £1 = $1.4.

	$ million
Dassault Mirage III	6.0-7.0
Northrop F-5E	8.0
Dassault Mirage F1	9.0-11.0
Northrop F-20	11.5
General Dynamics F-16	14.5
Tornado IDS	18.5
McDonnell Douglas F-18	21.0
Dassault Mirage 2000	23.0
Tornado ADV	23.3
McDonnell Douglas F-15	29.0
Grumman F-14	32.7

Above: ZA254, the first Tornado ADV prototype, over the Blackpool seafront and its famous tower during a test sortie from BAe's Warton airfield. Two further prototypes joined the test fleet in 1980.

Timescale comparison

A more valid criticism of Tornado is that of timescale. The case is best summed up in the form of a chart comparing the pace of Tornado with that of the F-14, F-15, F-16, F-18 and Mirage 2000. The result reflects very badly on the pace of European aircraft programmes, and should be framed and hung on the wall of every design office, production department and ministry involved in the new tri-national European Fighter Aircraft.

What I most emphatically do not want to suggest is that the engineers and designers employed by BAe, MBB, Aeritalia, and all the many companies which make up the Tornado industrial team have been dragging their heels. Several factors combine to make European aircraft plants less efficient than their US counterparts, and to build headwinds into European programmes.

Probably the best description of these is contained in a report prepared for the USAF by Rand, a leading US military think-tank. In their report *Multinational Co-production of Military Systems*, authors Michael Rich, William Stanley, John Birkler and Michael Hesse concentrate on the European F-16 programme, but the lessons also apply to Tornado.

US companies hire and fire personnel as required by the demands of a programme. Aerospace workers find it relatively easy to move from job to job, given the lack of red tape surrounding house purchase in the USA, and the ample availability of rented accommodation. In Western Europe moving house is not so easy, and a change of aerospace employer could even involve a change of country and language. A worker moving from GD to McDonnell Douglas could well be re-united with former colleagues, but BAe probably has few ex-Dassault employees. Since the workforce is less mobile, companies try to maintain a near-even level of employment. Full and continuous employment is more important than peak production rate.

Shift work is common in US aerospace, but European plants work more than one shift only in the cases of capital-intensive processes. European employees enjoy longer holidays, and often a shorter working week. One US company cited in the Rand report claimed that its employees worked 255 more hours per year than their European counterparts.

US plants are capital-intensive, supporting high production rates with a less skilled workforce. In Europe, employee skills are higher, and more labour-intensive production methods are used. The last-mentioned factor has in the past proved a problem when attempting to licence-produce a system devised on one side of the Atlantic in factories on the other side.

The pace of flight testing also tends to be slower in Europe than in the USA. For a start, European winter weather can ground flying operations at regular intervals. Another factor is that fewer aircraft are used in development during European programmes. In the case of the F-15, a fleet of 18 aircraft clocked up more than 3,000 hours of flight testing in two and a half years to prepare the

Right: ZA267, second ADV prototype, in formation with a Nimrod AEW.3, with which the type will operate when deployed in operational service with RAF interceptor squadrons.

aircraft for operational service. The numerically smaller Tornado test fleet took five years to reach 3,000 hours.

Tornado's development programme was once described as having proceeded at "glacial" pace. The adjective, although unkind, is accurate. Could the programme have moved faster? US employment practices are not acceptable in Western Europe, but shift working could have been applied at least to prototype design and construction. The general contraction of the aircraft industry in the mid-1960s should have made skilled personnel available, and salaries and wages could have been increased to compensate for social disruption. The result could have been the creation of a European equivalent of Kelly Johnson's Lockheed Skunk Works.

The charge that Tornado is overexpensive must be roundly dismissed, but the extended timescale does provide grounds for concern. The pace of the US F-15 programme, which was started the same year as Tornado but placed operational hardware in service five years earlier, suggests that the Skunk Works approach could have flown MRCA prototypes in 1972 instead of 1974, while multi-shift pre-series assembly could have resulted in early-production examples (probably built with Skunk Works help) in the hands of the TTTE by 1975 or 1976.

Below: ZA283, the third ADV prototype, in formation with a BAC Lightning interceptor, another Warton product and one of the types it is scheduled to replace in RAF service during the late 1980s.

Structure

The airframe of Tornado was designed to cope with the punishing stress of low-level high-speed flight, and the tri-national design team did a good job, the aircraft being free of the structural problems that plagued the F-111. Made from conventional materials such as aluminium alloy, rather than the composites being used on an increasing scale on most contemporary fighters, Tornado could be built easily on existing machinery, and will pose few problems for maintenance personnel. Each nation builds its own portion of the aircraft, and each has its own final assembly line.

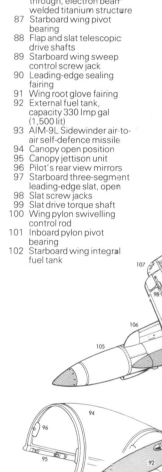

Above: Tornado ADV in combat air patrol (CAP) configuration displays its leading edge wing slats and fuselage-mounted airbrakes as it slows almost to stalling speed for the benefit of the photographer in the tail door of a C-130 Hercules.

Although designed a few years too early to make significant use of carbon-fibre and other advanced composites, Tornado seems none the worse for the lack of these. Instead it relies on conventional materials such as aluminium alloy and titanium. The structure has been designed for a long fatigue life, and incorporates a large number of access panels, accounting for 45 per cent of the total surface area.

The fuselage is of conventional design, and is made largely from aluminium alloy. The need to house a complex radar system in the nose dictated the use of a relatively large cross-section for the fuselage which, seen from the front, is near square in section with a wide, flat under-surface, the ideal location for external stores. Three hard points on this lower surface can be used to mount stores pylons.

Most of the fuselage structure is made up from closely spaced, integrally machined frames, longerons and skins. Wherever possible internal systems are positioned to be partially protected from ground fire by heavy items of structure such as frames and longerons. The APU and other secondary power system components are housed in an easily accessible location just aft of the centre-fuselage end frame.

The nose section is built by BAe. Mounted ahead of the cockpit section is an avionics compartment, and a double-hinged circular section housing the radar. The nose radome is the responsibility of AEG Telefunken (assisted by Aeritalia and BAe), and swings to starboard to give access to the radar during maintenance.

The canopy over the cockpit was designed to give a good view from both crew positions while still giving good protection against bird strikes. It is a single-piece unit manufactured by Kopperschmidt/AIT. Lucas Aerospace provides the windscreen and curved side panels, and these components in-

Maintenance access panels

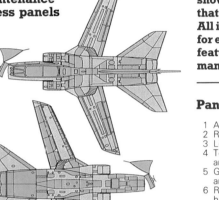

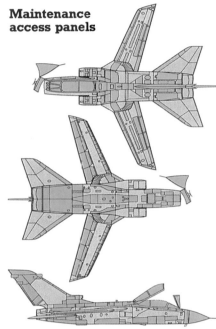

corporate a Sierracote electrically-conductive film able to supply the heat needed for de-icing and internal-surface demisting.

Each crew member has a Martin-Baker Mk 10A rocket-assisted ejection seat. These fully-automatic escape aids, developed from the earlier Mk 9, are cleared for operation from zero speed to Mach 2, and from ground level to 50,000ft (15,000m). If the crew need to eject the canopy is lifted clear of the aircraft by the power of two small rocket motors, but should it fail to jettison a miniature detonating cord is provided to shatter the transparency.

Below: Although sub-assembly manufacturing facilities are not duplicated, each of the three Panavia partner nations has its own final assembly line. This is the MBB line, showing early production aircraft.

Left: The yellow areas in this drawing show the sections of the aircraft's skin that can be removed for maintenance. All internal subsystems are arranged for easy removal and replacement, a feature conspicuously absent from many earlier patterns of jet fighter.

Panavia Tornado IDS (RAF GR.1) cutaway

1. Air data probe
2. Radome
3. Lightning conductor strip
4. Terrain following radar antenna
5. Ground mapping radar antenna
6. Radar equipment bay hinged position
7. Radome hinged position
8. IFF antenna
9. Radar antenna tracking mechanism
10. Radar equipment bay
11. UHF/TACAN antenna
12. Laser Ranger and Marked Target Seeker, starboard side
13. Cannon muzzle
14. Ventral Doppler antenna
15. Angle of attack transmitter
16. Canopy emergency release
17. Avionics equipment bay
18. Front pressure bulkhead
19. Windscreen rain dispersal air ducts
20. Windscreen
21. Retractable telescopic in-flight refuelling probe
22. Probe retraction link
23. Windscreen open position, instrument access
24. Head-up display
25. Instrument panel
26. Radar head-down display
27. Instrument panel shroud
28. Control column
29. Rudder pedals
30. Battery
31. Cannon barrel
32. Nosewheel doors
33. Landing/taxiing lamp
34. Nose undercarriage leg strut
35. Torque scissor links
36. Twin forward-retracting nosewheels
37. Nosewheel steering unit
38. Nosewheel leg door
39. Electrical equipment bay
40. Ejection seat rocket pack
41. Engine throttle levers
42. Wing sweep control lever
43. Radar hand controller
44. Side console panel
45. Pilot's Martin-Baker Mk 10 ejection seat
46. Safety harness
47. Ejection seat headrest
48. Cockpit canopy cover
49. Canopy centre arch
50. Navigator's radar displays
51. Navigator's instrument panel and weapons control panels
52. Foot rests
53. Canopy external latch
54. Pitot head
55. Mauser 27mm cannon
56. Ammunition feed chute
57. Cold air unit ram air intake
58. Ammunition tank
59. Liquid oxygen converter
60. Cabin cold air unit
61. Stores management system computer
62. Port engine air intake
63. Intake lip
64. Cockpit framing
65. Navigator's Martin-Baker Mk 10 ejection seat
66. Starboard engine air intake
67. Intake spill duct
68. Canopy jack
69. Canopy hinge point
70. Rear pressure bulkhead
71. Intake ramp actuator linkage
72. Navigation light
73. Two-dimensional variable area intake ramp doors
74. Intake suction relief doors
75. Wing glove Krüger flap
76. Intake bypass air spill ducts
77. Intake ramp hydraulic actuator
78. Forward fuselage fuel tank
79. Wing sweep control screw jack
80. Flap and slat control drive shafts
81. Wing sweep, flap and slat central control unit and motor
82. Wing pivot box integral fuel tank
83. Air system ducting
84. Anti-collision light
85. UHF antennas
86. Wing pivot box carry-through, electron beam welded titanium structure
87. Starboard wing pivot bearing
88. Flap and slat telescopic drive shafts
89. Starboard wing sweep control screw jack
90. Leading-edge sealing fairing
91. Wing root glove fairing
92. External fuel tank, capacity 330 Imp gal (1,500 lit)
93. AIM-9L Sidewinder air-to-air self-defence missile
94. Canopy open position
95. Canopy jettison unit
96. Pilot's rear view mirrors
97. Starboard three-segment leading-edge slat, open
98. Slat screw jacks
99. Slat drive torque shaft
100. Wing pylon swivelling control rod
101. Inboard pylon pivot bearing
102. Starboard wing integral fuel tank

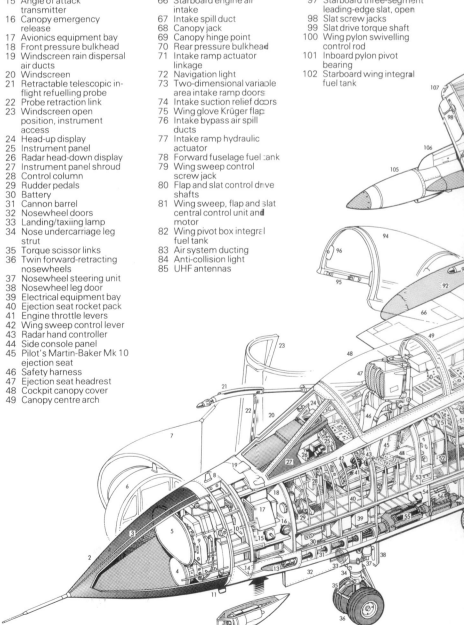

A Command Ejection mode has been provided for use during high-speed flight at low level. If this is selected, and the pilot decides to initiate ejection, the escape systems will first eject the navigator. If the navigator ejects, the front seater will not normally be affected, but the design of the escape system includes a lever in the rear cockpit which may be used to select Command Ejection mode. (As will be recounted later, this option for the navigator to eject the pilot was destined to result in at least one front-seater making an undignified and unnecessary departure from his aircraft.)

A Teddington air-conditioning temperature-control system automatically maintains the cockpit temperature between 41° and 86°F (+5° to +30°C). Marston provides the air-conditioning intercooler and Normalair-Garrett the precooler and cold-air unit, while oxygen is supplied by a Normalair-Garrett/Draegerwerk/OMI system.

Cockpit pressurization starts to take effect at 5,000ft (1,500m). The pressurization system is fed by air tapped from the HP compressor of the RB.199 engines, then cooled by heat-exchangers. As well as maintaining the cockpit environment, it supplies the air needed by the ventilated suits and anti-g suits of the crew, the windscreen and canopy demisting systems and the canopy seals.

The canopy seals help to reduce the level of noise in the cockpit, an important feature in an aircraft which is designed to spend much of its time in high-speed low-level flight. During early flight tests the noise level in the cockpit was found to be higher than anticipated, a fault eventually traced to vibration of the cockpit weather stripping at certain airspeeds, and a simple modification cured the problem.

MBB builds the fuselage centre section, including the wing inboard section. The latter has a leading-edge sweep of 60°, and incorporates a small Krüger flap in its leading edge. Mounted within the inboard wing section is the wing box used to carry the wing pivots and to transfer wing loads to the fuselage, coping with the large and variable bending and torsional moments created by the outer wing sections. It also acts as one of the aircraft's fuel tanks.

Wing carry-through box
When designing the F-111 back in the early 1960s, General Dynamics engineers decided to play safe, choosing D6AC steel as a structural material and assembling the box by means of precision bolts. This conservative choice did not prevent problems: by 1968 cracks were being found around the bolt holes, and GD were adding a 500lb reinforcing gusset to each box; a year later one aircraft and its crew were lost when the wing came off an aircraft engaged in carrying out a low-level attack.

For Tornado, the box is built from titanium and assembled not by bolts but by electron-beam welding (EBW). This operation is carried out in a chamber containing a powerful electron gun able to bombard the component under fabrication with a powerful current. This welding operation is carried out in a vacuum in order to prevent atmospheric gases from contaminating the resulting weld and causing cracking at a later date. The resulting component is lighter and stronger than an equivalent steel box would have been.

In the initial stages of the wing-box programme, MBB turned to Grumman for assistance. The latter had been experimenting with electron-beam welding of titanium and other materials since the early 1960s: having designed and built an experimental box-beam structure in the late 1960s, then tested this to destruction at 112 per cent load factor, the Long Island company had invested heavily in EBW equipment, and were using this technology to create the titanium wing box of the US Navy's F-14 Tomcat fighter. The first two prototype boxes were therefore assembled to MBB's design by Grumman, while the German company installed EBW equipment at its Ottobrunn plant.

103 Wing fuel system access panels
104 Outboard pylon pivot bearing
105 Sky Shadow ECM pod
106 Outboard wing swivel ing pylon
107 Starboard navigation and strobe lights
108 Wing tip fairing
109 Double-slotted Fowler-type flaps, extended position
110 Flap guide rails
111 Starboard spoilers, open
112 Flap screw jacks
113 External fuel tank tail fins
114 Wing swept position trailing edge housing
115 Dorsal spine fairing
116 Aft fuselage fuel tank
117 Fin root antenna fairing
118 HF antenna
119 Heat exchanger ram air intake
120 Starboard wing fully swept back position
121 Airbrake, open

122 Starboard all-moving tailplane (taileron)
123 Airbrake hydraulic jack
124 Primary heat exchanger
125 Heat exchanger exhaust duct
126 Engine bleed air ducting
127 Port airbrake rib construction
128 Fin heat shield
129 Fin integral fuel tank
130 Vortex generators
131 Fin integral fuel tank
132 Fuel system vent piping
133 Tailfin structure
134 ILS antenna
135 Fin leading edge
136 Forward passive ECM housing
137 Fuel jettison and vent valve
138 Fin tip antenna fairing
139 VHF antenna
140 Tail navigation light
141 Aft passive ECM housing
142 Obstruction light
143 Fuel jettison
144 Rudder

145 Rudder honeycomb construction
146 Rudder hydraulic actuator
147 Dorsal spine tail fairing
148 Thrust reverser bucket doors, open
149 Variable area afterburner nozzle
150 Nozzle control jacks (four)
151 Thrust reverser door actuator
152 Honeycomb trailing edge construction
153 Port all-moving tailplane (taileron)
154 Tailplane rib construction
155 Leading-edge nose ribs
156 Tailplane pivot bearing
157 Tailplane bearing sealing plates
158 Afterburner duct
159 Airbrake hydraulic jack
160 Turbo-Union RB199-34R Mk 101 afterburning turbofan engine

161 Tailplane hydraulic actuator
162 Hydraulic system filters
163 Hydraulic reservoir
164 Airbrake hinge point
165 Intake frame/production joint
166 Engine bay ventral access panels

167 Engine oil tank
168 Rear fuselage fuel tank
169 Wing root pneumatic seal

170 Engine driven accessory gearboxes, port and starboard, airframe mounted
171 Integrated drive generator (two)
172 Hydraulic pump (two)
173 Gearbox interconnecting shaft
174 Starboard side Auxiliary Power Unit, APU
175 Telescopic fuel pipes
176 Port wing pivot bearing
177 Flexible wing sealing plates
178 Wing skin panelling
179 Rear spar
180 Port spoiler housings
181 Spoiler hydraulic actuators
182 Flap screw jacks
183 Flap rib construction
184 Port Fowler-type double-slotted flaps, extended position
185 Port wing fully swept back position
186 Wing tip construction
187 Fuel vent
188 Port navigation and strobe lights
189 Leading-edge slat rib construction
190 Sky Shadow ECM pod
191 Outboard swivelling pylon
192 Pylon pivot bearing
193 Front spar
194 Port wing integral fuel tank
195 Machined wing skin/stringer panel
196 Wing rib construction
197 Swivelling pylon control rod
198 Port leading-edge slat segments, open
199 Slat guide rails
200 External fuel tank
201 Inboard swivelling pylon
202 Inboard pylon pivot bearing
203 Missile launch ra l

204 AIM-9L Sidewinder air-to-air self-defence missile
205 Port mainwheel, forward retracting
206 Main undercarriage leg strut
207 Undercarriage leg pivot bearing
208 Hydraulic retraction jack
209 Leg swivelling control link
210 Telescopic flap and slat drive torque shafts
211 Leading-edge sealing fairing
212 Krüger flap hydraulic jack
213 Main undercarriage leg breaker strut
214 Mainwheel door
215 Landing lamp
216 JP233 airfield attack weapon (two, side-by-side)
217 Submunitions compartments (30 SG357 runway penetration bombs and 215 HB876 area denial weapons in each JP 233)
218 Port shoulder pylon
219 Fuselage shoulder pylon (two)
220 ML twin stores carriers
221 BL 755 cluster bombs (eight)
222 Mk 83 high speed retarded bomb
223 Mk 13/15 1,000lb (450kg) HE bomb

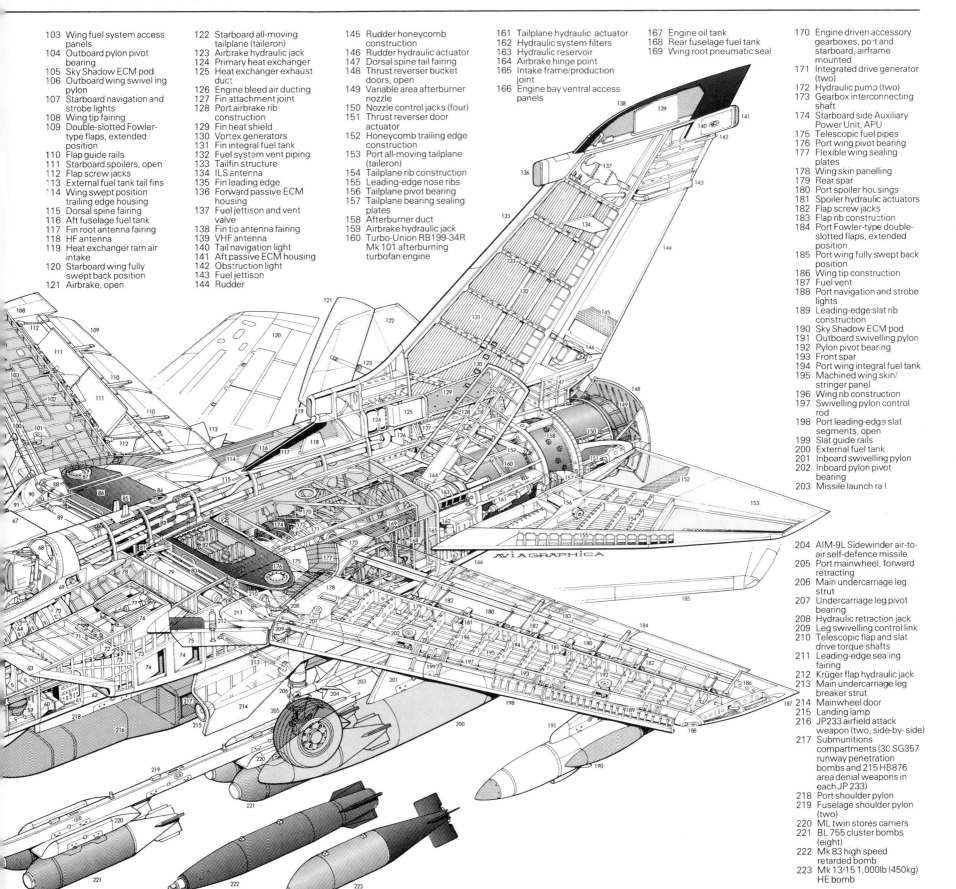

Wing sweep angles

Wing sweep angle varies from 25°
at speeds of up to Mach 0.73 to a
maximum of 67°.

45°
to Mach 0.88

58°
to Mach 0.9

67°
above Mach 0.9

25° to Mach 0.73

The outboard wing panels are pivoted hydraulically on Teflon-coated bearings. The pivot points are just outboard of the fuselage sides, and wing sweep may be varied through leading edge sweep angles ranging from 25° to 68°. As the wing moves to the rear its trailing edge slides into pockets in the fuselage centre section. Inflatable elastic seals close the gap between the wing and fuselage at all sweep angles, ensuring smooth aerodynamic contours and minimizing drag.

The wing is moved by re-circulating ball-screw actuators powered by hydraulic motors. One is fitted on each side of the centreline, and the two are interconnected by a synchronizing shaft able to transmit the drive from one to the other should one hydraulic system fail. The system is designed to ensure that both wings move in exact synchronization – if their angle varies by more than 0.5° the system will lock. The only embarrassing failure reported to date involved an Italian trainee pilot, who had the novel experience of seeing the cockpit wing-sweep control lever break off when he tried to move the wings forward for landing. The aircraft landed safely at a higher touchdown speed suited to the partially swept wings.

The outer wings are manufactured from aluminium alloy by Aeritalia, the upper and lower skins and their integral stiffeners being milled from single slabs of alloy. Piaggio provide the slats, wing leading edge and front spar, while SIAI-Marchetti build the wing root trailing edge, lower trailing-edge inspection doors, and wing tips.

Tornado is not fitted with ailerons, allowing the entire length of the wing to be devoted to lift-enhancing leading- and trailing-edge devices. Full-span leading-edge slats are fitted, three sections per side. The entire length of the trailing edge is taken up by double-slotted Fowler flaps arranged in four sections per side. Spoilers are provided to augment roll control by the tailerons. Two are located on each wing, and may be deployed after touchdown to dump wing lift and improve braking.

Four basic angles of wing sweep are normally used: 25° at speeds of up to Mach 0.73, 45° up to Mach 0.88, 58° to Mach 0.9 and 67° at higher speeds. Flaps and slats are available only at 25°, slats alone at 45°. At all greater angles slats and flaps are retracted.

Each wing is fitted with two stores pylons. Manufactured by Aermacchi, these are designed to swivel in flight, maintaining the fore-and-aft alignment of the ordnance, tanks or pods which they carry as wing sweep is altered. This swivelling movement is controlled by a system of rods and levers.

Above: Visible in this view of an RAF 27 Sqn machine are the double-slotted trailing-edge Fowler flaps, taileron position markings, engine exhaust warnings and the pneumatic seals over the wing root retraction housing. Power for undercarriage retraction is from the No 2 hydraulic system.

Intake construction

The air intakes are of horizontal-wedge type, and are mounted on the forward frame of the fuselage centre section. Movable ramps and actuators are located in the upper surface, and two blow-in doors on the sides. The air-intake control system is the result of a joint effort by Nord-Micro Electronic Feinmechanik, BAe, and Microtecnica, while Dowty Boulton-Paul and Liebherr Aerotechnic supply the intake ramp-control actuators. Intake de-icing equipment is the responsibility of AEG Telefunken.

Ducts running rearward from the intakes and curving in toward the centreline carry the air backward to the engine bays. Located in the BAe-built rear fuselage, these house the twin RB.199 powerplants, mounted side by side directly under the vertical tail, separated by a titanium firewall and protected by a Graviner fire-detection and extinguishing system. Two large load-carrying doors are incorporated so that engines may be lowered directly out of the airframe. Many fighters rely on engines being withdrawn to the rear, but this manoeuvre would be difficult to accomplish within the cramped confines of a hardened aircraft shelter of the type used at NATO's West European air bases. Two spade-type hydraulically-operated airbrakes are located on the fuselage shoulders directly above the engine bays, while the rear fuselage also incorporates the structural attachment points for the tail surfaces, the arrester hook and its uplock.

The all-moving horizontal tail surfaces (tailerons) are manufactured by BAe and operate in two modes, providing roll control by differential movement, pitch control by movement in unison. Tornado moves against the current fashion in fighter design by having a single vertical fin, whose area is dictated by the control demands of highly-manoeuvrable supersonic flight.

Right: An RB199 turbofan is manoeuvred into position before being hoisted into the engine bay of P.12. This photograph gives a good view of the titanium firewall that separates the two engines; also visible are the load-carrying doors which form the lower surface of the bays.

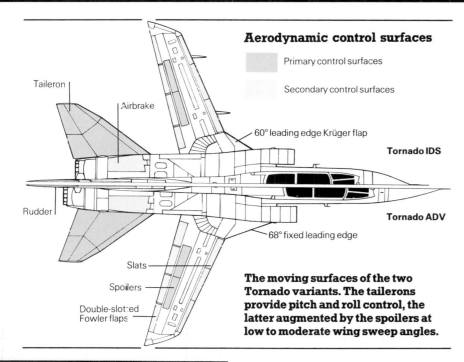

Aerodynamic control surfaces

Primary control surfaces

Secondary control surfaces

60° leading edge Krüger flap

Tornado IDS

Tornado ADV

68° fixed leading edge

Taileron

Airbrake

Rudder

Slats

Spoilers

Double-slotted Fowler flaps

The moving surfaces of the two Tornado variants. The tailerons provide pitch and roll control, the latter augmented by the spoilers at low to moderate wing sweep angles.

One significant difference between the tail of Tornado and that of the earlier F-111 is that the former's horizontal surfaces are positioned much lower on the fuselage than those of the US aircraft. On the F-111, the two surfaces are the same height. When Soviet designers tackled the MiG-23 'Flogger' and Su-24 'Fencer', the US layout was slavishly copied, the tailplane being at the top fo the fuselage and directly in line with the wing. Soviet designers are not normally reluctant to go their own way in the field of aerodynamics (sometimes with notable success, as in the case of the MiG-21-style tailed delta), but apparently did not foresee the aerodynamic problems which this tail position creates. Tornado and the Grumman F-14 were the first operational VG designs in which the horizontal stabilizer was placed lower on the fuselage, a formula which allows the airflow from the wing to help preserve the flow across the tail.

The single vertical fin is also made by BAe, contains an integral fuel tank, and carries a fairing for the ESM antennas. An inlet in the base of the fin supplies ram air to a heat-exchanger. Overall size

Below: Tornado's wing is the responsibility of Aeritalia: this view of the company's production line shows the assembly jigs. Those visible in the foreground are designed to rotate, giving good access to both sides of the partially assembled wing during the final stages of construction.

of the vertical fin is dictated by the control demands of a Mach 2 design, whereas most of Tornado's contemporaries feature the alternative solution of twin vertical tails, although the F-14 almost ended up with a single fin.

All control surfaces are hydraulically actuated. Tornado has two fully-duplicated hydraulic systems driven by Vickers hydraulic pumps on the engine gearboxes, and incorporating Dowty pressure accumulators and a Teves power pack. Both systems operate at 4,000psi (281kg/m²), the pressure pioneered by the UK on the Britannia airliner and Vulcan bomber a quarter of a century earlier.

Hydrulic power is used by the flying controls, with Fairey Hydraulics supplying the control surface actuators (taileron, rudder and spoiler). The flaps, slats, wing sweep, inlet ramps, undercarriage retraction, brakes, nosewheel steering and even the canopy actuators also use hydraulic power, and a valve is arranged to limit the flow rate to the wing actuators should a heavy demand from these approach the limit of what the system can deliver. Operation of the other systems is not degraded under such circumstances.

Actuation mechanisms for control surfaces and other moving parts are critical components on which the aircraft's safety will depend. Much detailed inspection is required for components such as the Tornado taileron actuators, which are machined from pre-stretched aluminium blanks. To improve throughput, Fairey Hydraulics invested in a PAG automatic inspeciton unit.

Undercarriage system

Tornado is designed to be able to operate from semi-prepared airstrips. The undercarriage and associated hydraulics are supplied by a team headed by Dowty Rotol, wheels, brakes and tyres are from Dunlop, and Goodyear supplied the anti-skid system. The twin-wheel steerable nose gear retracts forwards into a well located between the guns The main legs are of single-wheel type, and retract forwards and upwards into the fuselage. On prototype aircraft the nose wheel doors sometimes gave problems, tending to protrude under air loads at higher flight speeds. This was cured by strengthening the doors and their operating linkages. As noted above, an arrester hook is located beneath the rear fuselage.

The undercarriage actuators are connected only to the No. 2 hydraulic

system, but a bottle of high-pressure nitrogen is provided for emergency lowering purposes. A hand-pump is also provided, ensuring that there will always be sufficient pressure to operate the wheel brakes.

Tornado has a main 115/200V AC three-phase 400Hz electrical system, plus a 28V DC sub-system. Each of the two oil-cooled brushless electrical generators is able to supply most of the aircraft's power needs. Two fan-cooled transformer/rectifier units supply the DC power. In the event of a main electrical system failure a thyristor switching circuit will connect a battery able to supply emergency electrical power to essential services.

In theory the system is foolproof, but on September 27, 1983, a Tornado returning to RAF Honington after an uneventful night training sortie suffered a total electrical failure. One of the generators had failed, but the crew promptly reset it and carried on with the mission. Some 15 minutes later, as the aircraft was descending from its cruise height to 21,000ft (6,400m) the generator failed a second time. Moments later the navigator sensed a bright flash from the rear of the aircraft, a jolt and a sudden thump. All the aircraft's lights went out, and all systems (including the radio and intercom) began to fail.

The crew were reduced to having to unfasten their oxygen masks and yell at one another in an attempt to maintain communications. The pilot tried to fly the aircraft out over the coast, but soon told the navigator that he was losing control of the aircraft. Shortly afterward he ordered the navigator to eject. The navigator replaced his oxygen mask, lowered his visor, then ejected. The pilot failed to eject, and was killed when the aircraft crashed.

Training flights were temporarily halted pending an investigation. Analysis of the incident revealed that one generator had indeed come off line, and that AC and DC power had failed a few seconds later. Both engines had oversped to their governed limits – the inevitable outcome of a total power failure – and the turbines had mechanically failed and run down to windmilling speed. This failure accounted for the shock and flash reported by the navigator, but the cause for such a massive power failure could not be determined. The design of the electrical system was reviewed, and a number of modifications were made to the electrical system to improve reliability and redundancy.

More than half the internal fuel capacity of around 1,690 Imp gal (6,400 lit) is provided by self-sealing Uniroyal bag tanks in the centre fuselage, the remainder by the wing integral tanks and the wing box. Each wing tank has a single-ended AC booster pump which feeds fuel to the main tank groups. Fuel is gravity fed through non-return valves to the collector boxes – small tanks able to supply the engine during a limited amount of inverted flight. Two double-ended AC pumps, each powerful enough to feed the engines at full reheat at sea level, pass the fuel to the engine feed lines. Eichweber supplies the capacitance fuel-gauging system, Marconi Avionics the fuel-flow metering system. Refuelling is via a single NATO-pattern connection.

In 1983 Lear Siegler received a contract from Panavia worth $27 million to supply more than 2,500 external fuel tanks for use on Tornado. These may be carried on the two shoulder pylons and the two inboard wing pylons.

The RAF was the only IDS customer to require in-flight refuelling, so this was made an add-on extra in the form of a detachable flight-refuelling probe which may be fitted to the right-hand upper shoulder of the forward fuselage. This is not of the clumsy fixed type used on many RAF aircraft, but takes the form of a retractable unit mounted in a fairing which extends horizontally just below the canopy. On command from the cockpit, the probe is extended under hydraulic power. A buddy refuelling pod may be carried on the centreline so that one aircraft may refuel another.

ADV modifications

The basic structure described above required minimal modification to create the Royal Air Force's Tornado ADV interceptor. One change stemmed from the RAF's specifying a level of radar performance approaching that of the AWG-9 radar of the US Navy's F-14 fighter. Since the resulting radar set would be larger than the Texas Instruments multi-role radar fitted to Tornado IDS, the nose section of the aircraft had to be stretched to create the required internal avionics volume, and a new radome devised to match the operating frequency of the new set. Engineers replaced the relatively blunt shape used on the IDS with a more elongated design.

Primary long-range armament of the new interceptor would obviously be the BAeD Sky Flash – initially the Mk 1 version fitted to RAF Phantoms, but later the improved Mk 2. The simplest method of fitting these missiles to Tornado would have been to mount them on underwing pylons, rather than semi-flush beneath the fuselage (the carriage method used on the F-4 Phantom), but this created problems.

Since most of the Tornado wing lies outboard of the wing pivots, the pylons would have to swivel. Such a movement would increase the difficulty of maintaining accurate alignment of the missile's centreline with that of the fuselage, while the aerodynamic drag created by wing pylons would reduce the aircraft's performance to below that of the existing Phantoms. Semi-flush mounting would eliminate both difficulties, only to raise another – the fuselage of Tornado was too short to allow four rounds to be carried in this location.

The solution was another stretch of the forward fuselage, inserting a new section just aft of the cockpit. The effect of this can be seen by observing the position of the upper lip of the intake relative to the cockpit canopy. On the IDS, the lip falls directly below the frame at the canopy mid-point but on the ADV the upper lip is well aft of the frame. The two stretches total 4ft 5in (1.36m), and dictated minor modifications to other items of structure.

The sweep angle on the wing inboard fixed section was increased from the 60° used on the IDS to a new value of 68° on the ADV, and the small Krüger flap built into the IDS leading edge was deleted. These changes moved the wing centre of pressure forward, compensating for the fact that the fuselage stretch had moved the aircraft centre of gravity.

Although these changes reduced the degree of strandardization between the interceptor and strike versions, it introduced two significant gains. Internal fuel capacity could be increased by 10 per cent – an extra 200 gallons (910 litres) – and additional space was made available for avionics bays in the lower front fuselage, while the more elongated design displayed a lower supersonic drag (and thus promised a higher supersonic acceleration) than the standard Interdictor/Strike version.

The fuselage of the ADV, like that of the IDS, is of conventional design, and made largely from aluminium alloy. Introduction of the fuselage stretch did not create any manufacturing problems, but the larger radar and other items of avionics meant that additional heat had to be dissipated. To cope with this, the ADV is fitted with an extra heat-exchanger.

In developing the ADV cockpit, BAe made large-scale use of mock-ups, lighting rigs and other aids. The result was a cockpit in which the displays are ideally placed for viewing, and the controls and switches are easily reached. A further aid which aircrew will appreciate is that the wing sweep angle is varied automatically by the flight-control system to match aircraft angle of attack. Wing sweep and flap/slat position cover the same range of angles as on the IDS.

Right: Despite its Mach 2 top speed, Tornado handles well at low speed, as shown by this photograph taken from the tail door of a C-130. The aircraft's full span wing slats and flaps rival in high-lift effectiveness those fitted to airliners.

Fuel stowage

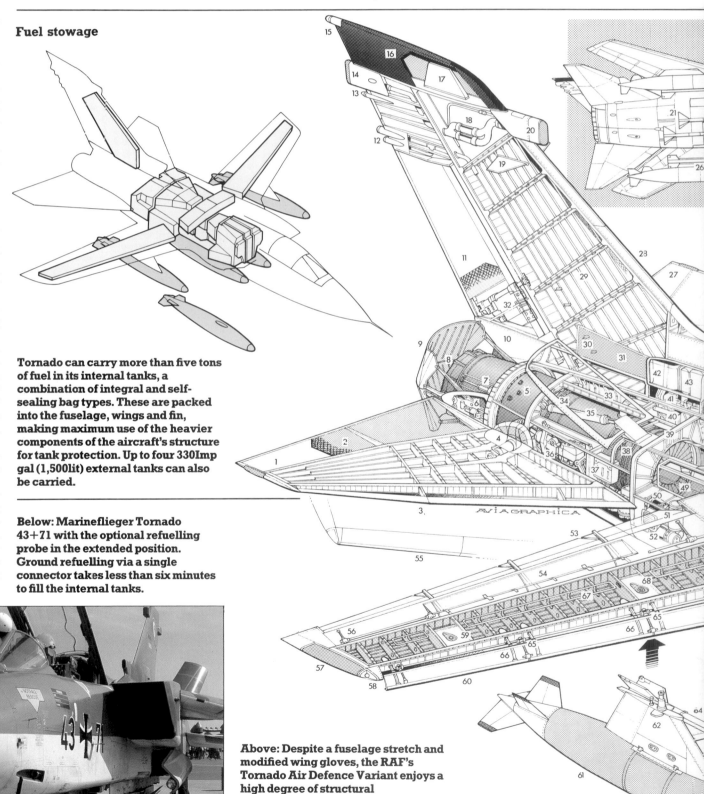

Tornado can carry more than five tons of fuel in its internal tanks, a combination of integral and self-sealing bag types. These are packed into the fuselage, wings and fin, making maximum use of the heavier components of the aircraft's structure for tank protection. Up to four 330Imp gal (1,500lit) external tanks can also be carried.

Below: Marineflieger Tornado 43+71 with the optional refuelling probe in the extended position. Ground refuelling via a single connector takes less than six minutes to fill the internal tanks.

Above: Despite a fuselage stretch and modified wing gloves, the RAF's Tornado Air Defence Variant enjoys a high degree of structural commonality with the basic Interdictor/Strike version. Comparison of this drawing with the IDS cutaway on pages 16/17 shows how minimal the internal changes have been – good news for RAF ground crews.

Panavia Tornado ADV (RAF F.2) cutaway

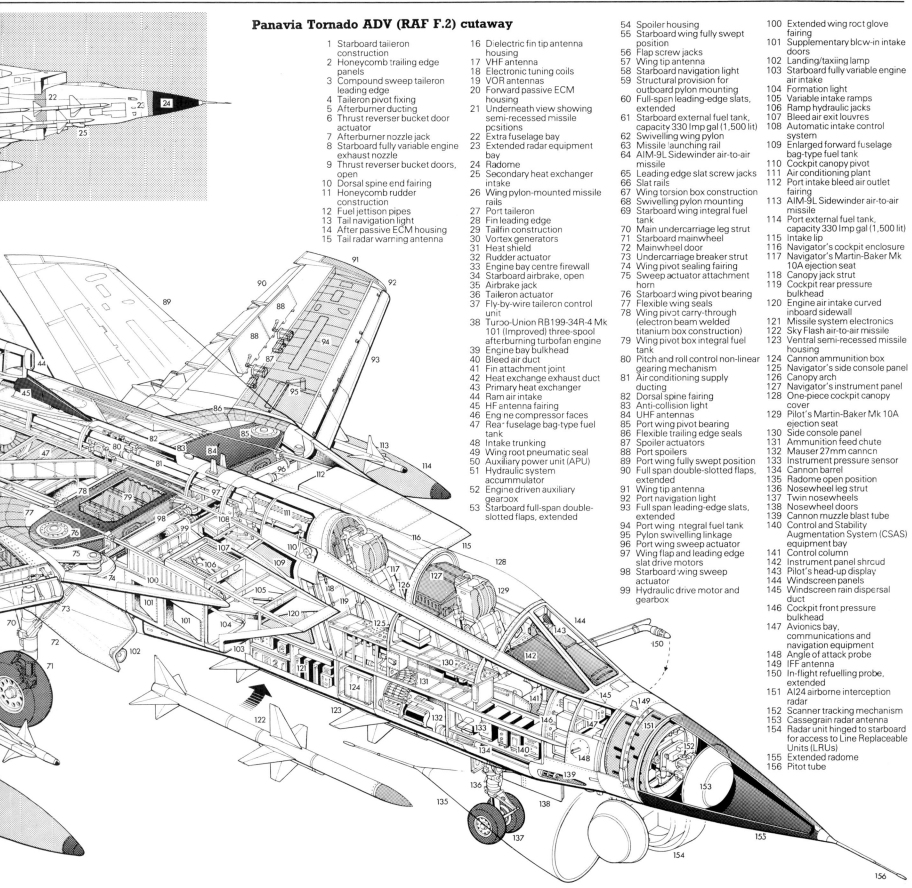

1 Starboard taileron construction
2 Honeycomb trailing edge panels
3 Compound sweep taileron leading edge
4 Taileron pivot fixing
5 Afterburner ducting
6 Thrust reverser bucket door actuator
7 Afterburner nozzle jack
8 Starboard fully variable engine exhaust nozzle
9 Thrust reverser bucket doors, open
10 Dorsal spine end fairing
11 Honeycomb rudder construction
12 Fuel jettison pipes
13 Tail navigation light
14 After passive ECM housing
15 Tail radar warning antenna
16 Dielectric fin tip antenna housing
17 VHF antenna
18 Electronic tuning coils
19 VOR antennas
20 Forward passive ECM housing
21 Underneath view showing semi-recessed missile positions
22 Extra fuselage bay
23 Extended radar equipment bay
24 Radome
25 Secondary heat exchanger intake
26 Wing pylon-mounted missile rails
27 Port taileron
28 Fin leading edge
29 Tailfin construction
30 Vortex generators
31 Heat shield
32 Rudder actuator
33 Engine bay centre firewall
34 Starboard airbrake, open
35 Airbrake jack
36 Taileron actuator
37 Fly-by-wire taileron control unit
38 Turbo-Union RB199-34R-4 Mk 101 (Improved) three-spool afterburning turbofan engine
39 Engine bay bulkhead
40 Bleed air duct
41 Fin attachment joint
42 Heat exchange exhaust duct
43 Primary heat exchanger
44 Ram air intake
45 HF antenna fairing
46 Engine compressor faces
47 Rear fuselage bag-type fuel tank
48 Intake trunking
49 Wing root pneumatic seal
50 Auxiliary power unit (APU)
51 Hydraulic system accumulator
52 Engine driven auxiliary gearbox
53 Starboard full-span double-slotted flaps, extended
54 Spoiler housing
55 Starboard wing fully swept position
56 Flap screw jacks
57 Wing tip antenna
58 Starboard navigation light
59 Structural provision for outboard pylon mounting
60 Full-span leading-edge slats, extended
61 Starboard external fuel tank, capacity 330 Imp gal (1,500 lit)
62 Swivelling wing pylon
63 Missile launching rail
64 AIM-9L Sidewinder air-to-air missile
65 Leading edge slat screw jacks
66 Slat rails
67 Wing torsion box construction
68 Swivelling pylon mounting
69 Starboard wing integral fuel tank
70 Main undercarriage leg strut
71 Starboard mainwheel
72 Mainwheel door
73 Undercarriage breaker strut
74 Wing pivot sealing fairing
75 Sweep actuator attachment horn
76 Starboard wing pivot bearing
77 Flexible wing seals
78 Wing pivot carry-through (electron beam welded titanium box construction)
79 Wing pivot box integral fuel tank
80 Pitch and roll control non-linear gearing mechanism
81 Air conditioning supply ducting
82 Dorsal spine fairing
83 Anti-collision light
84 UHF antennas
85 Port wing pivot bearing
86 Flexible trailing edge seals
87 Spoiler actuators
88 Port spoilers
89 Port wing fully swept position
90 Full span double-slotted flaps, extended
91 Wing tip antenna
92 Port navigation light
93 Full span leading-edge slats, extended
94 Port wing integral fuel tank
95 Pylon swivelling linkage
96 Port wing sweep actuator
97 Wing flap and leading edge slat drive motors
98 Starboard wing sweep actuator
99 Hydraulic drive motor and gearbox
100 Extended wing root glove fairing
101 Supplementary blow-in intake doors
102 Landing/taxiing lamp
103 Starboard fully variable engine air intake
104 Formation light
105 Variable intake ramps
106 Ramp hydraulic jacks
107 Bleed air exit louvres
108 Automatic intake control system
109 Enlarged forward fuselage bag-type fuel tank
110 Cockpit canopy pivot
111 Air conditioning plant
112 Port intake bleed air outlet fairing
113 AIM-9L Sidewinder air-to-air missile
114 Port external fuel tank, capacity 330 Imp gal (1,500 lit)
115 Intake lip
116 Navigator's cockpit enclosure
117 Navigator's Martin-Baker Mk 10A ejection seat
118 Canopy jack strut
119 Cockpit rear pressure bulkhead
120 Engine air intake curved inboard sidewall
121 Missile system electronics
122 Sky Flash air-to-air missile
123 Ventral semi-recessed missile housing
124 Cannon ammunition box
125 Navigator's side console panel
126 Canopy arch
127 Navigator's instrument panel
128 One-piece cockpit canopy cover
129 Pilot's Martin-Baker Mk 10A ejection seat
130 Side console panel
131 Ammunition feed chute
132 Mauser 27mm cannon
133 Instrument pressure sensor
134 Cannon barrel
135 Radome open position
136 Nosewheel leg strut
137 Twin nosewheels
138 Nosewheel doors
139 Cannon muzzle blast tube
140 Control and Stability Augmentation System (CSAS) equipment bay
141 Control column
142 Instrument panel shroud
143 Pilot's head-up display
144 Windscreen panels
145 Windscreen rain dispersal duct
146 Cockpit front pressure bulkhead
147 Avionics bay, communications and navigation equipment
148 Angle of attack probe
149 IFF antenna
150 In-flight refuelling probe, extended
151 AI24 airborne interception radar
152 Scanner tracking mechanism
153 Cassegrain radar antenna
154 Radar unit hinged to starboard for access to Line Replaceable Units (LRUs)
155 Extended radome
156 Pitot tube

Powerplant

Combining an untried engine of innovative design with a new airframe was a massive gamble of the sort that gives aircraft designers sleepless nights, but in the case of Tornado one which paid off handsomely. Still the only three-shaft combat turbofan, the Turbo-Union RB199 is more compact than other engines in its thrust class, and plays a vital role in providing the speed and range that the customers had demanded. Had Panavia opted to take the safer course of using a two-shaft engine, the resulting aircraft would have been bigger and heavier, and its story perhaps somewhat duller to recount.

Above: Most of the load-bearing doors which form the lower surface of the engine bays were not installed when this view of the sixth prototype was taken. Note the compact size of the twin afterburners – testimony to the skill of the RB199 design team.

When the decision to develop Tornado was taken back in 1969 no off-the-shelf European powerplant was available to meet the demanding specification. The powerplant was required to have a high dry thrust for good transonic performance, high afterburning thrust for takeoff, air combat and supersonic dash, and a low specific fuel consumption. If this were not enough, planners also asked for a rapid throttle response, specifying that the engine spool up from flight idle to maximum dry thrust in only four seconds, and required the engine to be able to operate in full afterburner for long periods – as much as 35 minutes for some missions.

Not surprisingly, US engine makers Pratt & Whitney (P&W) and General Electric (GE) tried to capture what would clearly prove a lucrative order. The obvious P&W contenders were advanced derivatives of the TF30 engine used in the General Dynamics F-111 and planned for the Grumman F-14 Tomcat, but the company also offered the JTF16 (an engine which existed only on paper) and the newer JTF22, which would eventually become the USAF's problem-dogged F100. GE's candidate was the GE/1/10 design.

The prospect of the aircraft having a European engine were not good. Rolls-Royce's contemporary military afterburning engines were the obsolete Avon turbojet used in the Lightning interceptor, the new afterburning version of the Spey, which was creating problems on the RAF and Royal Navy versions of the Phantom, and the very much smaller Rolls-Royce/Turboméca Adour being developed for Jaguar. The abandoned Anglo-French Variable Geometry Aircraft would have used a two-shaft M45G turbofan proposed by Bristol Siddeley and SNECMA, but development of this engine was ended by SNECMA after the collapse of the AFVG programme. SNECMA's Atar series of turbojets was of similar vintage to the Avon, while the M53 turbofan now used in the Mirage 2000 was still at the earliest stages of design.

If the MRCA was to have a European engine a new design would be needed. An earlier UK study of a future fighter had looked at a Bristol Siddeley BS.143 two-shaft engine combining the LP and HP spools of existing engines. In 1966 Rolls-Royce took over Bristol Siddeley. Working in conjunction with the Bristol engineers and those from the fighter design team at Warton, Rolls-Royce had examined existing engines and even existing "paper" engines, concluding that none adequately met the new requirement. Looking beyond the technology used in the M54G engine, designers investigated the possibility of using the three-shaft layout which Rolls-Royce's Derby engineers had created for the RB211 civil turbofan, and this turned out to be the key to the problem of powering the new fighter.

Two factors which have a large influence on engine efficiency are the turbine entry temperature (TET) – the temperature at which the hot gases leave the combustion chamber – and the overall pressure ratio of the compressor section. TET is largely controlled by the materials from which the turbine's early stages are manufactured, while pressure ratio is a function of compressor design.

Early jet engines were of the single-shaft configuration, with compressors and turbine mounted on a common shaft and rotating at the same speed. There is a limit to the amount of compression which can be generated from a single stage: if this figure is pushed too high, the blades of the compressor will be operating closer to the stall, reducing the engine's surge margin and making it more difficult to handle.

Early jet engines such as the de Havilland Goblin, using simple centrifugal compressors, managed a compression ratio of around 3.3; TET was around 1,470°F (800°C), and the engine burned almost one and a quarter pounds of fuel for every pound of thrust produced. (This last figure is known as specific impulse and is a good measure of engine efficiency.) Centrifugal-flow engines were

Above: A Rolls-Royce technician works on an RB199's mated intermediate-pressure (IP) and high-pressure (HP) sections, whose outer casing encloses the bypass duct.

Below: The swivel test rig at Manching in Germany is used to check engine operation at all attitudes. Oil is injected into the efflux to make the exhaust pattern visible.

based on British wartime design concepts and were soon made obsolete by better engines with multi-stage axial compressors. An early example of the latter type was the P&W J47 used in the F-86 Sabre: this had a 12-stage axial compressor with an overall compression ratio of 4.8:1, a TET of 1,600°F (711°C) and an SFC of 1.1.

SNECMA's Atar 8K5C and 9K50 are typical present-day examples of single-shaft turbojets. Each has a nine-stage compressor which manages a modest 6.15:1 pressure ratio. The Rolls-Royce Viper 600 is similar, managing a pressure ratio of 5.8:1 from an eight-stage compressor. TETs are much higher than on first-generation engines.

Engines of this type are able to generate a thrust equal to four or five times their own weight at full afterburner, and SFC is lower than that of the older centrifugal type – for the Atar it is 0.97, rising to 1.96 when the afterburner is lit.

General Electric's widely used J79 turbojet does its best to overcome the limitations of single-shaft construction by having variable-geometry stators mounted on the engine casing in a manner which allows them to be adjusted in much the same way as the blades of a variable-pitch propeller, these enable the engine to be matched to varying operating conditions. The 17-stage compressor manages an overall compression ratio of 13.4:1, and the TET is around 1,800°F (983°C), a value typical for turbojets designed in the 1950s. The J79 develops almost five times its own weight when running in full afterburner, while SFC is 0.85 dry, 1.98 with afterburner.

SFC figures for full afterburner are largely independent of the efficiency of the engine – the massive increase in thrust is obtained by pouring fuel into the afterburner at a prodigal rate – and the hallmark of engine efficiency is dry SFC, a parameter which falls as engines improve. For every pound of dry thrust generated, the Atar burns only 88 per cent of the fuel that a J47 would demand, while the J79 makes do with only 77 per cent.

The first two-shaft engines were created in 1949 by Pratt & Whitney and

Bristol Engines. Designers split the compressor and turbine sections of the engine into separate high-pressure (HP) and low-pressure (LP) sections, each with its own shaft, so that each was free to rotate at the speed which would give optimum performance. The degree of compromise inherent in compressor blade design was thus reduced, resulting in a higher compression ratio from a smaller number of stages – or higher performance from a more compact powerplant.

The P&W J52 was broadly in the same performance class in dry thrust as the J79, managing a respectable 14.5:1 pressure ratio and an SFC of 0.88, but achieving these figures with only 12 compressor stages (five LP stages plus seven HP stages) rather than the 17 of the J79. This type of engine would have a brief life in the West as a fighter powerplant, as the combination of two-shaft construction and the turbofan principle was to provide still further improvement in engine performance.

First two-shaft afterburning turbofan was the P&W TF30. On the P-414 version which currently powers the Grumman F-14, a three-stage fan and six-stage LP compressor, plus a seven-stage HP compressor, give an overall pressure ratio of 17.5:1; better materials allowed a TET of just over 2,000°F (1,090°C).

Single-shaft engines were not made obsolescent overnight. Their relative simplicity ensured continued use even to the present day in classic designs such as the SNECMA Atars which power the Mirage III, Mirage 5, Mirage 50 and Mirage F1, the General Electric J85 in the T-38 and F-5, the General Electric J79 used to power the Lockheed F-104 Starfighter, McDonnell Douglas F-4 Phantom and IAI Kfir, the Lyulka AL-7, -9 and -21 used in many Sukhoi fighters, and the Rolls-Royce Avons fitted in the BAC Lightning.

The two-shaft configuration has dominated military engine design to the present day. When SNECMA took the conservative step of retaining a single-

shaft configuration when developing its new M53 military turbofan in the late 1960s, this was almost certainly the last time that the configuration would be adopted for a major new military engine: barring unforeseen developments in engine technology, the multi-shaft concept now rules supreme. When designing its new M88 engine for the Dassault Rafale fighter, SNECMA adopted a two-shaft layout.

Three-shaft concept

The three-shaft configuration took the concept of sub-dividing the rotating parts of an engine into optimized sections a stage further, adding a third intermediate-pressure (IP) section to the compressor and turbine. The RB211 was shorter than rival two-shaft designs, and although in theory it was more complex than a two-shaft design, Rolls-Royce engineers claimed that the move to a three-shaft configuration had in fact reduced the number of components.

Rolls-Royce may have been a firm believer in the three-shaft principle, but both Pratt & Whitney and General Electric continued to back two-shaft designs. One measure of the boldness of the three-shaft scheme is that despite the success of the RB211, the only nation apart from the UK to have selected the three-shaft configuration for high-bypass engines is the Soviet Union. The Lotarev bureau used a three-shaft layout for the D-36 powerplant of the Antonov An-72 'Coaler' STOL jet transport and Yak-42 airliner, and repeated the formula when creating the 51,650lb (23,500kg) thrust D-18T turbofans of the Antonov An-124 'Condor'.

By the early summer of 1968 Rolls-Royce had decided that the best candidate for what was then MRCA was a three-shaft afterburning turbofan. The result was the RB199, which proved so superior to the US offerings that a go-ahead was given in October 1969, and Turbo-Union was formed to manage the design, development and manufacturing tasks. Turbo-Union is a tri-national consortium directed by a board of representatives from each of the partner companies. The headquarters is at Filton on the outskirts of Bristol in the UK, while the main operating plants are those of Rolls-Royce (Filton, England), Motoren und Turbinen-Union (Munich, West Germany) and Fiat Aviazione SpA (Turin, Italy).

Rolls Royce and MTU both had a 40 per cent share in development work, with Fiat handling the remaining 20 per cent, while the division of production work reflects the total engine buy of each partner – Rolls-Royce 47.7 per cent, MTU 39.9 per cent and Fiat the balance of 12.4 per cent.

As with the airframe, all three partners have their own final assembly lines, but each nation is responsible for individual sections of the powerplant. Rolls-Royce is responsible for the LP compressor,

Below: An RB199 runs at full afterburner on a test stand at Rolls-Royce's Bristol plant. With the afterburner at full augmentation thrust of the Mk 101 is almost doubled.

Above: An RB199 is prepared for installation in the first MRCA prototype. Initial taxiing trials carried out in early 1974 relied on non-flight-rated engines.

TURBO-UNION RB199 Mk 101	
Length	127in (323cm)
Weight	1,980lb (900kg)
Diameter	34¼in (87cm)
Intake	Annular, no inlet guide vanes
Air flow	154lb/sec (70kg/sec) approx
Bypass ratio	c.1:1
LP fan	Three-stage
IP compressor	Three-stage
HP compressor	Six-stage
Combustor	Annular, with vaporizing burners
Turbine-inlet temp	2,240°F (1,227°C)
HP turbine	Single-stage air-cooled
IP turbine	Single-stage air-cooled
LP turbine	Two-stage uncooled
Max thrust (dry)	8,090lb (36kN)
Max thrust (afterburning)	15,950lb (71kN)

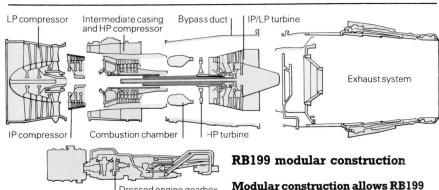

LP compressor — Intermediate casing and HP compressor — Bypass duct — IP/LP turbine — Exhaust system

IP compressor — Combustion chamber — HP turbine

Dressed engine gearbox

- Rolls-Royce (UK)
- MTU (West Germany)
- Fiat Aviazione (Italy)

RB199 modular construction

Modular construction allows RB199 assemblies to be replaced at wing maintenance level; engine modules are interchangeable, and rotating parts do not need re-balancing.

combustor chamber, HP turbine, turbine casing, and afterburner, MTU builds the IP and HP compressors, IP turbine, intermediate casing and gearbox, bypass duct and thrust reverser, while Fiat tackles the LP turbine and shaft, rear bearing support, exhaust diffuser and rear jet pipe.

Engine operating conditions

A critical decision which the designers had to make was the operating conditions for the new engine. We have already seen how increased pressure ratios made possible by the the two-shaft principle, higher operating temperatures permitted by improved materials, and the use of the turbofan principle, had greatly improved engine efficiency. This process had continued through the late 1960s and early 1970s.

In designing the new F100 for the USAF's F-15 Pratt & Whitney aimed at ambitious targets. Bypass ratio of the new engine was fixed at 0.7:1, while a three-stage fan and 10-stage HP compressor were used to obtain a pressure ratio of 17.8:1, and TET was no less than 2,565°F (1,407°C). These ambitious figures gave a dry SFC of 0.69 at normal rating and 0.71 at Military Intermediate power, and the F100 can generate a thrust of 8.28 times its own weight. But P&W had almost bitten off more than they could chew: if the TF30 had hit development problems, the F100 had them in spades, with early engines

suffering short component lives and proving vulnerable to stalling.

One fact which must be borne in mind is that the RB199 and F100 were designed to cope with very different operating conditions. The task of the Tornado powerplant is to drive the aircraft through the sky at treetop level faster than possible pursuers can fly. The latter include the MiG-21, -23, -29 and -31, plus whatever Rostisav Belyakov can get off the drawing board and into the air during the life of the aircraft. The F100 was designed for dogfighting – probably the most difficult environment imaginable, requiring an engine able to tolerate vicious throttle slams and to drive the Eagle through violent air-combat manoeuvres. Those P&W designers at Palm Beach are among the best in the business, and they were pushing the turbofan technology of the late 1960s to its limits.

For the RB199, the Turbo-Union team decided to aim for an overall pressure ratio of 23:1, generating this by means of a three-stage fan, three-stage intermediate-pressure compressor and a six-stage HP compressor. Average pressure rise per stage would thus be an ambitious 1.3:1, well above the 1.2:1 of the TF30 and 1.25:1 of the F100, but lower than the 1.33 to 1.38 achieved by more recent US engines the F404 achieves an overall pressure ratio of 25:1 by means of a three-stage fan and seven-stage HP compressor, while the F101 and its F110

derivative manage 27:1 and 30:1 with nine HP compressors and two- and three-stage fans respectively. In choosing the TET for the new engine, the designers were less bold than their P&W counterparts, opting for 2,240°F (1,227°C) – a value between that of the established TF30 and the bold target set for the F100.

The resulting engine was an unqualified success: still the world's only known three-shaft afterburning engine, it remains unsurpassed in compactness and light weight. The current Mk 103 weighs around 1,980lb (900kg) and develops 16,920lb (75.26kN) of thrust – 8.5 times its own weight. The only engine likely to match this figure is the F404, with a ratio of 8.0 in early models but the promise of 17,000lb (75.6kN) or even 18,000lb (80kN) in later versions.

Mating a new engine with a new airframe is often a recipe for technical problems. The RB199 certainly had its share of design problems, but these were to prove minor compared with those which affected some contemporary US engines.

Given the fact that the engine was needed to power an all-new fighter,

Below: This view of an engine on the test stand gives a good view of the burner rings. Early engines experienced surging problems, and the sight of aircraft with only one 'burner lit was not uncommon at air shows in the mid to late 1970s.

Turbo-Union would have ideally liked the engine programme to lead the airframe by one and a half or even two years. Instead, the consortium was given the go-ahead some six months after the aircraft. The only solution was to get engines running as soon as possible and to plan a phased series of improvements and refinements.

A batch of 16 development engines was built, the first running on the bench at Patchway for the first time on September 27, 1971. Eight ground test benches were built – four in the UK, three in Germany, and one in Italy – and by the end of 1972 engines were running in all three countries. Four altitude test rigs were also built, all in the UK, the engine commencing altitude trials for the first time in November 1972.

Flight trials began on April 19, 1973 aboard a Hawker Siddeley Vulcan testbed. This aircraft had already been used to test the Olympus engine used by Concorde, so it was available complete with extensive instrumentation facilities, plus underbelly hard points for engine mounting. For the RB199 trials a full-size replica of one side of a Tornado fuselage was mounted beneath the fuselage of the bomber, ensuring that the engine would be running under realistic conditions, drawing its air from the planned design of intake and air ducting. The Vulcan could only expose the engine to speeds of up to Mach 0.92 and heights of up to 50,000ft (15,000m). Supersonic running had to be done in a test cell at the National Gas Turbine Establishment at Pyestock.

Two of the development engines were tested in the Vulcan. Built to RB199-01 standards, these were 11 per cent below nominal dry thrust, and 19 per cent low in full afterburner. Engines of this type were used to power the original prototypes of Tornado.

During early flight tests the RB199 displayed a distressing tendency to shed HP turbine blades. These losses never resulted in an engine malfunction – the crew were often unaware of any problem – and were cured by the introduction of modified blades.

By redesigning the IP and LP turbine blades engineers created a greater annulus area within the same casing, allowing a greater airflow through the engine. The resulting RB199-02 engine was first run in January 1974, and was flying in Tornado by August of that year. On bench test the -02 engine successfully demonstrated Formal Qualification Test specification dry and afterburning thrust, plus an SFC 5 per cent better than that of the -01 engine. Despite this, gas temperature had been reduced. By the summer of 1976 all seven of the Tornado prototypes which had been flown were fitted with engines modified to this improved standard, which was also known as RB199-34R.

Some flutter had been noted in the fan blades when the engine was running at high rpm in one part of the flight envelope. This was cured by the wider-chord fan blades which, along with modifications to the afterburner, led to the more powerful RB199-03. Engines of this standard were running on the bench by October 1974, and airborne in the Vulcan testbed in July 1976. First flight of a -03 engine in Tornado took place in March 1977.

Engine surge

One problem which was to dog the early models of engine was that of surging – the unstable breakdown of the flow of air and gas through the powerplant. This gives a characteristic explosive sound which can be heard over normal jet noise and even through the other noises of a Farnborough or Paris air show.

RB199 Mk 101

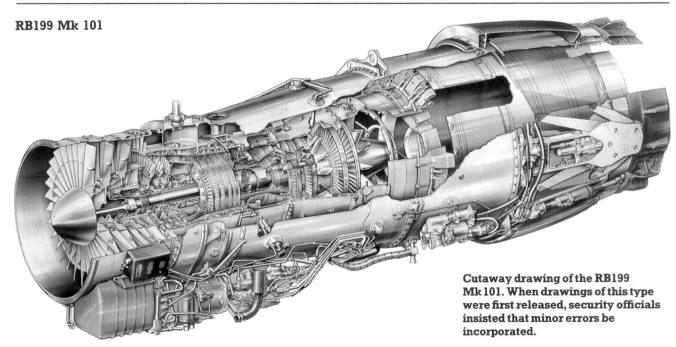

Cutaway drawing of the RB199 Mk 101. When drawings of this type were first released, security officials insisted that minor errors be incorporated.

Aviation journalists watching Tornado flight demonstrations during the late 1970s often whiled away the time with jokes about "winking" engines, speculating on the number of afterburners which would be lit on the next flypast. Turbo-Union put on a brave face, sometimes solemnly explaining to reporters that the aircraft on show had two engines of different build standard so that it sometimes looked as if only one burner was lit!

Such problems are an inevitable part of the development of any high-performance jet engine. All programmes suffer from them, but despite its novel three-shaft layout, the RB199 had fewer than were experienced by contemporary US engines such as the TF30 and F100.

Improved SFC and thrust were achieved by the RB199-04 version, which had more efficient compressors and turbines. This ran on the testbed in February 1977 and was airborne in the Vulcan in January of the following year, clearing the design for flight use. First Tornado to receive the new engine was the original prototype, which began flying under RB199-04 power in March 1978. The RB199-04 was the final variant

Right: The first ADV prototype (ZA254) with only one afterburner lit. At this late stage of the development programme (October 1978), the port side engine's dry thrust setting may have been deliberate, rather than the result of an engine surge.

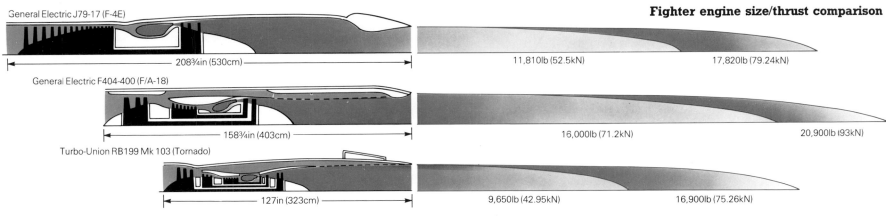

Fighter engine size/thrust comparison

General Electric J79-17 (F-4E)
208¾in (530cm) — 11,810lb (52.5kN) — 17,820lb (79.24kN)

General Electric F404-400 (F/A-18)
158¾in (403cm) — 16,000lb (71.2kN) — 20,900lb (93kN)

Turbo-Union RB199 Mk 103 (Tornado)
127in (323cm) — 9,650lb (42.95kN) — 16,900lb (75.26kN)

The RB199 and the General Electric F404 are similar in thrust to the GE J79 turbojet which powered the F-104 Starfighter and F-4 Phantom, but are much smaller. The efficient three-spool layout of the Turbo-Union engine results in its being significantly smaller than the F404, an engine developed on a slightly later timescale, and the compact dimensions of the RB199 frees more of Tornado's internal volume for fuel.

Left: This view of the RB199 (left) and J79 (right) graphically illustrates the effect of two decades of engine technology. Particularly notable is the greatly reduced size of the afterburner on the Turbo-Union engine.

to be developed before production began. In all, 51 prototype and pre-series engines were built, providing powerplants for the nine Tornado prototypes and six pre-series aircraft.

The -04 design formed the basis of the initial production engine. First of these new engines, which carried the service designation RB199 Mk 101, development design, were delivered in 1978, and were flying in Tornado by October of that year. Following successful FQT in November 1978, production deliveries began in 1979, and the engine entered service in July 1980.

The RB199 is in the same thrust class as the US J79 turbojet and its F404 turbofan replacement. The veteran J79 is 209in (530cm) long and weighs 3,847lb (1,745kg), while the use of modern technology on the later F404 brought the length of that engine down to 159in (403cm) and the weight to around 2,000lb (908kg). The Turbo-Union design team produced an even more compact engine only 127in (323cm) long, and managed to shave the weight down to 1,980lb

(900kg). The Mk 101 initial service model developed around 8,090lb (36kN) of dry thrust and 15,950lb (71kN) with after-burner.

The engine's compact size largely results from the use of three shafts. The outer shaft carries the low-pressure (LP) rotating parts – a three-stage fan and two-stage turbine. The intermediate shaft rotates in the opposite direction and carries a three-stage intermediate-pressure (IP) compressor and a single-stage turbine. The inner shaft rotates in the same direction as the outer, and has a six-stage HP compressor and a single-stage turbine. Air flow through the engine is approximately 154lb/sec (70kg/sec).

The intake of the engine is annular. Like most modern military powerplants it has no inlet guide vanes, but leads directly to the LP fan, a lightweight three-stage axial unit aerodynamically derived from that of Pegasus. The discs and blades are manufactured from titanium alloy and assembled by electron-beam welding, a technique which minimizes weight and reduces vibration.

Bypass ratio of the RB199 is approximately 1:1, half the fan air being ducted around the core section while the remainder enters the three-stage IP compressor. The rotor is mostly made from titanium alloy, with the individual discs

welded together and the blades secured by dovetail roots, and the casing is milled from titanium. An IP blow-off valve is provided to trim the airflow.

The HP compressor is of six-stage axial design with forward rotor blades manufactured from titanium, those at the rear from heat-resistant alloys. The stator blades are steel alloy.

Overall pressure ratio of the fan and compressors is 23.5:1, and the air from these passes into an annular combustor made from nickel-based alloy and fitted with vaporizing burners. Care has been taken to ensure near-complete combustion, maximizing efficiency and reducing smoke emission from the completed engine.

The hot gases from the combustor are fed directly to a highly-loaded HP turbine of single-stage configuration; the rotor blades and stator vanes are cast in heat-resistant nickel-base alloy then machined into shape. Since the HP turbine must cope with the 2,240°F (1,227°C) gas flow from the annular combustion chamber, the rotor and stator blades are air cooled. In addition to driving the HP compressor, the HP shaft also powers the engine and aircraft accessories. The IP shaft is driven by a single-stage IP turbine with air-cooled blades, while the LP shaft has a two-stage turbine with uncooled blades.

The hot efflux then passes through an exhaust diffuser and into the afterburner. In conventional afterburners core efflux is mixed with cooler air from the fan and bypass duct before being reheated, but the Turbo-Union team took the bold step of eliminating this section of the afterburner and re-heating both airflows at the same time, thus eliminating the mixing section of the afterburner and creating a more compact engine. Maximum gas temperature is approximately 2,995°F (1,625°C), and an air-cooled heat shield protects the jet pipe.

Afterburning thrust of a J79 engine is around one and a half times the dry rating – an augmentation of 51 per cent. Modern US engines such as the F100 and F404 have around 66 and 60 per cent augmentation respectively, but the RB199 managed a stunning 97 per cent in its original Mk 101 form.

The rear section of the afterburner incorporates a variable-area nozzle and twin-bucket thrust receiver. Care has been taken to minimize the base area of the convergent fully-variable final nozzle when the engine is running in dry thrust. (If this is not done, base drag in dry thrust can prove embarrassingly high. The Gloster Javelin was not known as the Dragmaster for nothing – according to aeronautical legend, the take-off performance of the afterburning version was inferior to that of the non-afterburning versions.)

On the RB199 four screw-jacks driven by air motor control the position of the translating ring – a movable outer shroud which drives the individual segments of the nozzle. The thrust-reverser is of the external, two-bucket type, whose upper and lower spades are driven by flexible shafts powered by a high-pressure pneumatic motor running on air bled from the engine's HP section.

A radial shaft transfers energy from the HP shaft to the secondary power systems (SPS). Each engine gearbox contains a hydraulic pump, an integrated constant-speed drive electrical generator (IDG) and pumps for oil and fuel. Engine and gearbox oil is cooled by a heat exchanger which transfers the heat to fuel drawn from the aircraft's tanks. This can be fed into the engine when fuel demand is high, but is otherwise routed back to the tanks via an air-cooling radiator.

The two engines are linked via their gearboxes by means of a cross shaft which is automatically engaged if the speed of the two powerplants differs by more than a specified value. A single engine may thus be used to drive both gearboxes and SP systems.

The gearbox of the right-hand engine in Tornado incorporates an auxiliary power unit (APU) manufactured by Kloeckner-Humboldt-Deutz, who also supply the starter. The APU burns fuel from the aircraft tanks and is started using the aircraft battery. It drives the right secondary power system gearbox and its associated hydraulic pump and electrical generator. Once APU power has been used to start the first engine via a gearbox torque converter, and the engine has reached idle power, the drive shaft of the RB199 takes over the task of driving the secondary power system, and the APU is automatically

Above right: An early development model of the RB199 is prepared for static test running. The spades of the thrust reverser are partially deployed above and below the nozzle.

Right: An RB199 engine about to be mated with its gearbox. The latter contains a hydraulic pump, oil and fuel pumps, and the electrical generator, and is cooled by fuel.

shut down. A cross shaft is then used to transfer power to the other gearbox, allowing the second engine to be started. If full electrical and hydraulic power is needed for ground testing, and the engines are not required, the APU may be used via the cross shaft to drive the SDS of both engines.

Control system

Building the engine was one thing, controlling it was another. Regulating the flow of fuel to the engine, and monitoring the response of those six spools – three per engine – became the task of the main-engine control system (MECU). This electronic unit accepts commands from the throttle, translating these into signals which control the hydromechanical engine and afterburner fuel systems and the nozzle actuation system, while monitoring the results via engine-mounted sensors.

The original MECU hit major development problems, delaying the delivery of flight-rated engines. Rolls-Royce urgently designed a replacement, which allowed the engine to be cleared for prototype flying. Rolls-Royce is not in the engine-control business, so production of the MECU was handled by another company.

To achieve the massive boost in thrust which the afterburner provides, the latter must be fed with large amounts of fuel, taking the SFC to 2.25. The SFC at dry thrust remains classified, but since the Lyulka and Tumansky bureaus will

have long since completed their own estimates, the estimation of an approximate figure is hardly likely to bring the defences of the Western world crashing down overnight. The obvious trick is to use existing engines as a yardstick.

The lowest SFC figures are those associated with the high-bypass ratio subsonic turbofans. Best result is the 0.37 of the TF34, a figure similar to that for the civil turbofans which power modern airliners. This is hardly surprising, since both have a bypass ratio of around 6:1. Afterburning military turbofans have a lower bypass ratio, and thus show poorer SFC figures:

Engine	Application	Bypass ratio	Dry SFC
RM8	Viggen	1.0	0.64
TFE 1042-7	(none)	0.84	0.7
Adour	Jaguar	0.75	0.74
F100	F-15	0.7	0.69
M53	Mirage 2000	0.35	0.87

A good clue to the likely performance of the RB199 is given by the RM8 and Adour. Given that the RB199 uses more recent technology than the JT8D-based RM8, we can confidently assign it an SFC at dry thrust of 0.6 to 0.65.

The Mk 101 entered production in 1978 and by the spring of the following year more than 50 had been delivered. The 200th example came off the line in December 1980 and by May 1982 total deliveries had reached 500.

Powered by the Mk 101, Tornado was able to enter service, but it was soon acknowledged that high-altitude fuel

consumption was exceeding the specifications. By the end of 1981 the technical press was reporting deficiencies in medium- and high-level performance, while initial service experience showed that the engine was not meeting the specified time-between-overhaul of 600 hours. In January 1983, the UK Comptroller and Auditor-General reported that all 417 engines delivered up to the end of 1982 had failed to fully meet the acceptance standards, but that acceptance of the Mk 101 standard had been necessary in order to avoid delays in Tornado production.

Turbo-Union acknowledged these problems, pointing out that a solution was already at hand in the form of the definitive RB199 Mk 103. This version first flew in Tornado in December 1981, and entered production in May 1983. It was used from Tornado production Batch 4 onward.

As well as proving more reliable, the Mk 103 also gave a useful thrust increase of between five and 12 per cent. This engine has an improved LP turbine with higher air mass flow and an aerobatic oil tank, the latter clearing the engine for sustained operation at negative or zero g and at extreme altitudes. Detail changes include the installation of a CUE 400 electronic control system, a redesign of LP turbine bearing housing, modifications of the bleed air system (including a new bleed valve in the IP compressor and removal of the outlet in the sixth stage of the HP compressor), improved internal seals to reduce air leakage, and a smokeless combustion system. Fuel consumption is reduced, and time between overhauls is greater. This is the current service version, and fully meets all specifications. Dry thrust is 9,656lb (42.95kN) rising to 16,920lb (75.26kN) in full afterburner. It was introduced on Batch 4 aircraft, but the RAF intends to upgrade 100 of the earlier Mk 101 to the Mk 103 standard by modification kits.

The German and Italian air arms decided to have their Mk 103 engine downrated to the same thrust as the Mk 101, and hoped in this way to gain an additional 30 per cent in TBO. By the summer of 1985 reliability of the Mk 103 in RAF service was slightly better than anticipated, with unplanned removals taking place at the rate of 5.3 per thousand flying hours instead of the expected 5.5.

Like most modern engines the RB199 can profit from the introduction of single-crystal blade technology, and an RB199 with around 90 single-crystal blades in the HP turbine started endurance testing at Rolls-Royce's Bristol facility in 1984. The new blades were designed to have an increased life span, and the bench tests – scheduled to run for about a month – were intended to prove whether they could be cleared for use in the Mk 103. There has been no subsequent news of this project.

Mk 104 for the ADV

The Tornado IDS was designed as a strike aircraft, but the ADV is a dedicated interceptor. Everyone knows the hoary old joke about the lost motorist who asks a passer-by for the directions to his destination, only to be told, "If I were you, I wouldn't start from here!". That was the problem which the ADV designers faced – the RB199 was not the ideal powerplant for an interceptor. The very qualities which make it a superb engine for an interdictor/strike aircraft work against it in the interceptor role.

This fact is a result of the engine's relatively high bypass ratio, which does wonders for SFC in subsonic cruise but becomes a penalty at higher speeds. The problem was once summed up in colourful language by British aviation

RB199 Mk 103

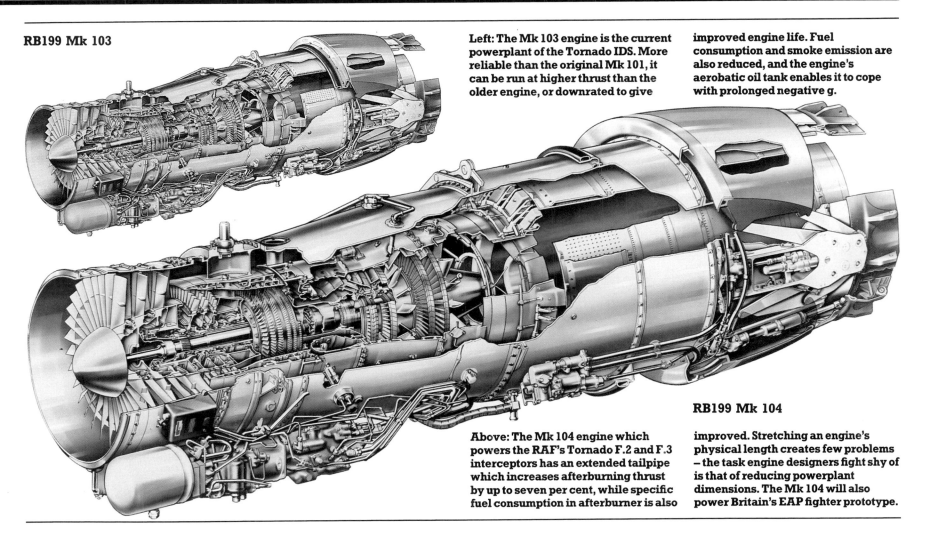

Left: The Mk 103 engine is the current powerplant of the Tornado IDS. More reliable than the original Mk 101, it can be run at higher thrust than the older engine, or downrated to give improved engine life. Fuel consumption and smoke emission are also reduced, and the engine's aerobatic oil tank enables it to cope with prolonged negative g.

RB199 Mk 104

Above: The Mk 104 engine which powers the RAF's Tornado F.2 and F.3 interceptors has an extended tailpipe which increases afterburning thrust by up to seven per cent, while specific fuel consumption in afterburner is also improved. Stretching an engine's physical length creates few problems – the task engine designers fight shy of is that of reducing powerplant dimensions. The Mk 104 will also power Britain's EAP fighter prototype.

writer Roy Braybrook – a man rarely short of a *bon mot* on any aerospace topic. His curiously-titled treatise on aero engine technology "Myself, Elizabeth Taylor and other fantasies", published in the magazine *Air International*, described the problems posed by high-bypass fighter engines. "As the aircraft's speed increases, the dry thrust of these engines goes down like lead at a shipwreck . . . the SFC is screwed as too much of the air being taken through a cycle of too low a pressure ratio".

For this reason the trend in supersonic turbofan design has been toward lower bypass ratios, except for powerplants intended for strike/bomber applications, such as the TF30, which has the same 1:1 bypass ratio as the RB199. In creating the later P-414 version for use in Tomcat, P&W reduced the bypass ratio to 0.9:1. Next came the F100 for the F-15 Eagle, in which the ratio fell to 0.7:1, while the F101 for the B-1 bomber used a ratio of 2:1. With the YJ101 engine for the YF-17 GE reduced the bypass ratio to a mere 0.2:1 – enough to improve subsonic SFC while earning the engine the epithet of "leaky turbojet". The production F404 derivative for the F-18 used a less radical 0.34:1. In designing the F110 derivative of the F101 GE engineers reduced the bypass ratio to 0.85:1 to match the new engine to the fighter role.

In the case of the ADV the budget probably did not permit radical F101/F110 style surgery; nor, one suspects, did the RAF desire engine commonality with the IDS. The bypass ratio would have to stay at 1:1, but greater thrust was required, particularly at altitude. To provide this Turbo-Union devised the uprated Mk 104 (originally known as the RB199ER). Longer than the earlier models, this is extended just aft of the afterburner flameholders by some 14in (36cm). Thrust is increased by up to seven per cent, but specific fuel consumption in afterburner is slightly improved. The first production batch of 18 ADVs will use the Mk 103, their airframes having been built before the decision was taken to use the longer Mk 104. The first run of an engine with the extended tailpipe came in March 1982.

Another feature of the Mk 104 is a Lucas Aerospace Digital Engine Control Unit (DECU). Intended to replace the Lucas CUE300 analogue control system on the current RB199 Mk 103 used by the Tornado IDS, the DECU had demonstrated repeatability and accuracy of performance in controlling the engine in both afterburning and dry modes during flight tests since February 1984.

Units of this type control the engine more accurately and consistently, allowing the powerplant to run closer to its ideal limits. Life-cycle costs can thus be reduced; Lucas estimates the savings likely from the installation of a DECU on the ADV as around £4.0 million over the life of the aircraft fleet.

Tornado IDS spends most of its life at low altitude, but the ADV must cope with all altitudes, or even indulge in zoom-climb tactics to deal with some high-flying targets. To cope with possible engine flame-outs at high-altitude, a retractable ram-air turbine is fitted. This will provide emergency power, and may be used to restart the engines. The ADV will also rely on tanker support to extend its range and endurance, so in place of the add-on probe used on the Tornado IDS, the ADV has a retractable probe housed in the port side of the forward fuselage.

By the time the Tornado production programme ends, more than 2,000 RB199 engines will have been delivered. By 1985 around half the engines required by the programme had already been built, and production was expected to run until 1989.

The Mk 104 is also being used to power the BAe Experimental Fighter Aircraft technology demonstrator due to fly in the summer of 1986, just after this book is published, but the planned European Fighter Aircraft will be powered by a new engine based on RB199 technology.

Right: RB199 assembly at Fiat Aviazione in Italy. By the time production ends in 1989, Rolls-Royce, Fiat and MTU will have delivered more than 2,000 engines.

Avionics

Tornado's payload of black boxes introduced the user air arms to a new level of avionics complexity, but are as essential to the success of the mission as any other part of the aircraft. Companies in all three nations pooled their talents to create systems as advanced as any in the world: the terrain-following radar keeps the aircraft safely down among the weeds, the nav/attack system gives levels of accuracy that crews of less well equipped types can only envy, and the cockpit displays present, in readily comprehensible format, all the data the crew will require during the mission.

When the MRCA programme was launched, the partner nations set up an industrial consortium known as Avionics Systems Engineering GmbH to develop and coordinate the aircraft's complex avionics suite. This would be responsible for sub-contracting the work to three national avionics consortia – EASAMS (Elliott-Automation Space and Advanced Military Systems) in the UK, EGS (comprising Standard Elektrik Lorenz, Rohde & Schwarz, Siemens, and Telefunken) in West Germany and SIA (Fiat, CGE-FIAR, Selenia, Marconi-Italiana, Societa Italiana Telecommunicazione, Siemens, Microtecnica Italiana, Montedel-Montecatini Edison Elettronica, and Filotecnica) in Italy.

This arrangement proved unworkable, so in 1971 EASAMS was given the prime contract and the task of sharing the work with EGS and SIA under suitable sub-contracts. The avionics testing activities of the flight test programme were managed by MBB.

Just as the RAF and Luftwaffe had found themselves backing different MRCA concepts (complex two-seat versus simpler single-seat), the two services had differing views of the proposed avionics suite. The UK regarded itself with justification as the leading source of European all-weather attack avionics expertise, and was determined to press for a complex and highly capable system; West Germany, still talking in terms of replacing its huge F-104G fleet on a near one-for-one basis, was interested in keeping price down and reliability high.

The obvious clash of opinion was over the navigation and attack system which, like all major Tornado systems, was the subject of an international design competition. The most sophisticated proposal came from Ferranti and Elliott in the UK, and would have involved the installation of three sensors – an I/J band terrain-following radar, a high-definition Ku-band attack radar designed for use during approach to the target, and a laser ranger for the final run.

The other candidates were of US design. Autonetics proposed an advanced radar using a first-generation electronically scanned antenna, while Texas Instruments used the experience gained in developing the APG-110 terrain-following radar of the F-111 in drawing up plans for a new set optimized for Tornado. Given the magnificent reliability which the F-111 terrain-following radar had displayed in operational service with the USAF, and the relatively low cost of TI's generally conservative proposal, the outcome was not hard to predict. TI got the job, which it shared with a European industrial team headed by AEG-Telefunken and including Elettronica, Ferranti, FIAR, Marconi and Siemens.

This use of US technology fuelled the fires of controversy, leading to political accusations that lack of design experience and manufacturing facilities in

Above: Key to Tornado's effectiveness, the radar system uses a large elliptical antenna for ground mapping and a smaller circular antenna below it for terrain following; both operate in Ku band.

West Germany and Italy would result in the US avionics industry dominating the MRCA programme, while the British laboratories which had developed the advanced nav/attack systems of the TSR-2 would be starved of work. It all sounded terribly dramatic at the time, with accusations that the UK would lose its expertise in advanced attack radars, but in retrospect the whole issue was something of a storm in a teacup. Tornado was an international programme and had to be developed internationally: no single nation could be allowed to hog a major portion of the action in order to support its own industrial interests.

NAMMA had the unenviable task of trying to share the work evenly between the participating nations, and in no area was this as difficult as in avionics. The process was protracted, injecting a delay of around six months into the programme, but was finally concluded satisfactorily.

Wherever possible, the avionics suite adopted by all customers was kept standard. In the early stages of the programme, the degree to which the suite would be adapted in order to meet individual national requirements must have alarmed the design team, but the need of maximum commonality eventually limited such national variations to communications, electronic warfare and the facilities needed to handle and release specialized weapons such as the MW-1 submunitions dispenser (Ger-

Above: All Tornado's avionic systems are designed to make maintenance simple. One example is the way the windscreen hinges forward to give access to the pilot's instrument panel.

Below: The E-scope display of the terrain-following radar shows the profile of the ground ahead of the aircraft, with a computer-generated ski-toe template superimposed.

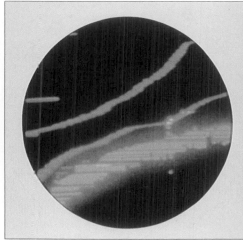

Terrain-following system

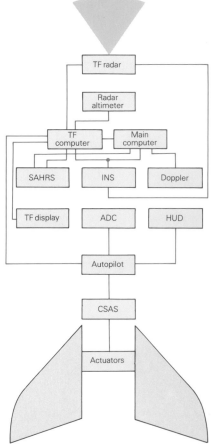

```
                TF radar
                   |
              Radar
             altimeter
                   |
     TF  ───────────────  Main
   computer            computer
        |                  |
  ┌─────┴─────┬──────┬─────┴─────┐
 SAHRS       INS          Doppler
                   |
 TF display       ADC          HUD
                   |
               Autopilot
                   |
                 CSAS
                   |
               Actuators
```

This block diagram depicts one of the most critical elements of Tornado's avionics – the terrain-following system used to fly the aircraft at low levels. Clearance height may be preselected, and the system can cope with speeds of up to Mach 1.2.

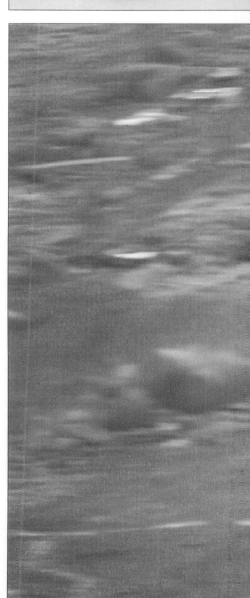

Terrain-following operation

The terrain-following system generates a theoretical ski-toe shaped envelope projected forward of the aircraft, and compares this with the profile of the terrain ahead. If the terrain penetrates the ski-toe trace, an automatic climb command is generated and passed to the autopilot and flight-director computers, resulting in an input to the control surfaces. Flight director commands are also passed to the pilot's head-up and head-down displays, and typical display indications are illustrated here.

E-scope display

1	2	3
Ground returns penetrate ski toe	Ground returns on ski toe	Ground returns below ski toe

HUD

| Pull-up command | Command satisfied | Push-over command |

Attitude direction indicator

Scan limits

Zero command line (ski toe)

0nm 1nm 2nm 3nm 4nm 5nm 6nm

---

many only) and the Kormoran anti-ship missile (Germany and Italy only).

One problem in documenting Tornado's avionics is that British electronics companies seem singularly vulnerable to changes of name. Elliott (a major supplier of Tornado systems) has during the life of the Tornado programme become Marconi Avionics then GEC Avionics, for example, while Marconi Space and Defence Systems has become Marconi Defence Systems. To

Below: A Tornado IDS from the TTTE banks right in a spectacular demonstration of low-level terrain-following flight during a sortie over North Wales in August 1984.

ease the problem for readers attempting to cross refer to earlier accounts of Tornado, this account will attempt to use the company name current when individual equipments were developed and put into production, but will try in the cases of major subsystems to note changes of name.

Avionics testbeds

Two Hawker Siddeley Buccaneer light bombers were rebuilt by Marshall of Cambridge in order to act as avionics testbeds. From November 1974 onward these subsonic aircraft were used to test-fly major items of avionics so that these would be available in proven form for installation in the two MRCA prototypes

assigned to avionics testing, Germany's 98+05 (formerly D-9592) and 98+06. Fourth and seventh prototypes respectively, they flew for the first time in September 1975 and March 1976. The first prototype to integrate the TI radar and other nav/attack systems with the digital autopilot and flight-control system, 98+05 provided the data needed to give the three Governments the confidence to order Tornado into production, while 98+06 was closer to the production standard and completed the task of proving the basic avionics suite.

Although commonly thought of as being a single radar, the TI set in the nose of Tornado actually comprises two radars sharing a common mounting,

power supply and processor/computer. Known as the Ground Mapping Radar (GMR) and the Terrain-Following Radar (TFR), both are broadband frequency-agile units operating in Ku-band rather than the lower frequencies in I/J band used by many airborne radars.

This dual radar introduced the user air arms to modern electronic technologies such as microwave integrated circuits (used in various amplifiers and oscillators) and surface acoustic wave (SAW) devices used in the pulse-compression and bandpass filtering systems. Solid-state signal sources known as Gunn diodes are used in the exciter master oscillator, the system that generates the signal which the radar amplifies to a high power level for transmission. They also act as the signal source in the local oscillator of the TFR receiver system.

A large elliptical antenna taking up most of the space within the radome is used by the ground mapping radar, while a smaller circular unit mounted immediately below it is associated with the terrain-following radar.

Tornado's survivability in combat would largely depend on the terrain-following radar (TFR). This equipment allows Tornado to fly at low level and at high speed, avoiding radar detection. Cruise height is defined by a "clearance" control whose settings range from 200 to 1,500ft (60-450m).

Like most terrain-following radars, the Tornado TFR monitors a ski toe-shaped flight envelope ahead of the aircraft, checking continuously to see whether any terrain or other feature protrudes above this and, if it does, generating an automatic climb command which may be either passed to the flight-control system or displayed on the pilot's HUD. The TFR antenna is circularly polarized in order to minimize the effects of weather on radar performance. In straight and level flight it carries out a two-bar scan pattern. If the aircraft

makes a turn, the antenna is steered into the turn. For small turns the scan pattern is opened out linearly in the appropriate direction; larger turns are handled by switching to a figure-of-eight scan pattern. The TFR thus gives the aircrew the ability to manoeuvre the aircraft while in terrain-following mode.

The ski-toe and the terrain ahead of the aircraft are shown to the pilot on an E-scope (slant range versus elevation angle) CRT display, enabling him to monitor the operation of the radar throughout the period of terrain-following flight, checking that no terrain features remain above the ski-toe for a significant length of time. In parallel with this human monitoring, the system also carries out a continuous process of cross-referencing and self-monitoring.

The system is able to cope with the maximum low-level speed of the aircraft, and hard, medium, or soft ride may be selected by means of a three-position switch. In the soft operating mode the flight-control system will limit the negative g forces experienced by the aircraft and its crew, giving relatively gentle climb and dive commands and limiting vertical acceleration increments to not more than −0.5g, but taking the aircraft higher above the terrain than would be desirable in close proximity to anti-aircraft threats. With hard ride selected the system will expose aircraft and crew to −0.95g increments in the vertical plane, holding the aircraft as close as possible to the profile of the terrain over which it is flying, and giving the lowest possible degree of exposure to anti-aircraft defences.

Ground mapping radar
The ground mapping radar is the primary attack sensor, and provides air-to-air and air-to-ground modes. Its planar-array antenna is a four-lobe monopulse unit which may be driven through wide and narrow scan patterns at fast and slow scanning speeds.

High-resolution ground mapping modes are used for accurate fixes to update the aircraft's navigation system, and to provide target identification. Normal operating mode is Ground Map Spoiled, which is used to give a general view of the terrain ahead of the aircraft.

Use of the word "spoiled" in no sense implies degraded performance, but rather reflects the technology of earlier-generation radars. The optimum beam shape for ground mapping is cosecant squared, which directs most of its energy along angles close to the centre-line, and greatly reduces the amount released at angles well away from the centreline. As a result, the distant terrain is illuminated by a powerful signal, while terrain at shorter range requires (and receives) much less radar energy.

In the days before phased-array antennas this beam shaping was achieved either by designing a customized antenna, or by fitting a retractable mechanical spoiler to a conventional antenna so that its normal beam shape could be modified to provide cosecant squared coverage when the set was being used in ground mapping mode. In the case of Tornado, this beam shaping is almost certainly accomplished by electronic manipulation of the phased-array antenna of the GMR, with the term "spoiled" being used to indicate "shaped for optimum ground mapping".

Ground Map Wide mode uses an earth-stabilized scan pattern to monitor a wide arc of the horizon, while Ground Map Narrow observes only a narrow sector, normally that towards which the aircraft is heading. As its name suggests, Ground Map Pencil mode uses a narrow pencil-like beam for target tracking and other specialized tasks.

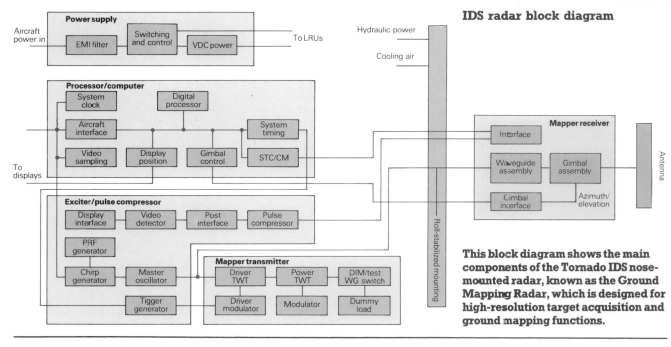

IDS radar block diagram

This block diagram shows the main components of the Tornado IDS nose-mounted radar, known as the Ground Mapping Radar, which is designed for high-resolution target acquisition and ground mapping functions.

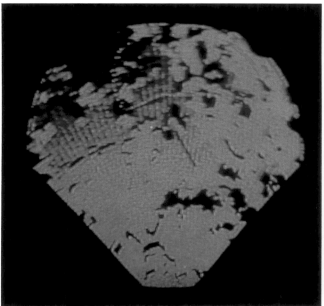

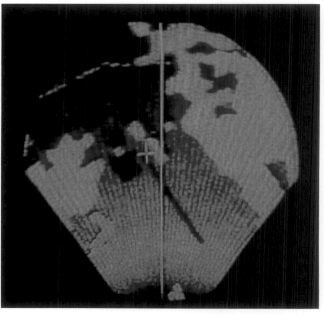

Above left: This typical Ground Mapping Radar display shows a target – an airfield runway – several miles ahead. The aircrew can now begin the attack sequence.

Above: At closer range the computed target marker position can be updated using the hand controller; the crew are then able to carry out a highly accurate non-visual attack.

When used in On-Boresight Contour Mapping mode, the GMR transmits a one-bar stabilized scan pattern, illuminating the terrain ahead. All terrain features below a chosen, zero-height, horizontally stabilized clearance plane are ignored, while any terrain features protruding above this height are displayed simultaneously with the ground map video. This mode provides a terrain-avoidance facility, allowing the aircraft to fly around rather than over terrain features while in low-level flight.

During the attack the GMR automatically acquires, locks on to and tracks designated ground targets. An Air-to-Ground Ranging mode allows the antenna to be pointed at ground targets, enabling the set to provide digital data such as target azimuth and elevation, slant range, and range rate.

Other operating modes are Height Finding (used against surface targets to provide the nav/attack system with data

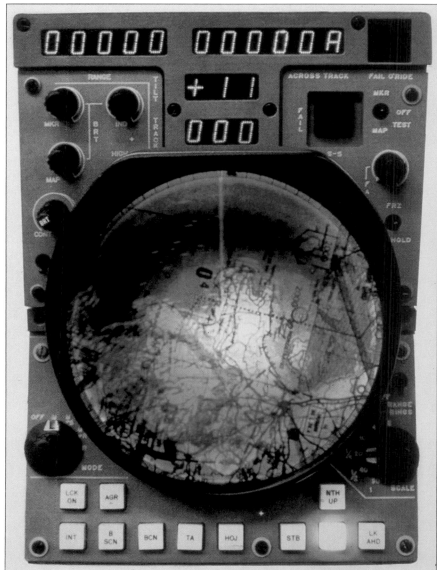

Left: Having identified the radar image of the target, the navigator can compare this with the computer-predicted position shown on his Combined Radar and Projected Map Display. Any error may be corrected.

for height computations), Home on Jam (a useful technique for use against hostile emitters), and Beacon (which locates and identifies friendly surface and air units by interrogating their radar beacons).

Tornado is primarily intended as a strike aircraft, but the radar does have an Air-to-Air Tracking mode. This allows the set to search for and lock on to aircraft targets such as hostile fighters or its own airborne refuelling tankers. Once acquired, the target is angle tracked unless rejected by the aircrew. If the signal is lost due to fading or jamming the radar will predict its position by extrapolating from previous returns.

Attempts to sell the aircraft on the export market indicated a need for better air-to-air capability. The result was the Radpac (radar package) scheme announced in April 1978. This used existing hardware modules to give the set a greatly-improved air-to-air capability without degrading its air-to-ground performance, but no further details of the scheme were released and there are no reports of its having been adopted by Tornado customers.

Fly-by-wire system

One of the most critical items of avionics is the fly-by-wire flight-control system, which introduced the Panavia partners to a new level of sophistication and complexity. Tornado was the first combat aircraft to enter production with an all-electric triplex fly-by-wire system.

The fly-by-wire system is a triplex (three-channel) analogue system, backed up by a mechanical system. In the mid-1980s, with digital electronics in the home in the form of microprocessor-controlled kitchen appliances, personal computers and Compact Disc players, the use of analogue electronics may seem unduly conservative, but back in 1974 when the Tornado was designed the choice of an analogue system reflected the state of the art. Similar configurations had already been flown on the BAe/Aérospatiale Concorde in 1969 and on a Royal Aircraft Establishment Hunter testbed in 1972. A digital system had been flight tested on a NASA F-8 in 1972 but this was singlex (single-channel) only.

Two years later GD designers were also to opt for analogue electronics when creating the F-16. Being inherently stable, Tornado was able to rely on a mechanical back-up, but the F-16's relaxed stability ruled out mechanical systems and dictated the use of quadruplex (four-channel) fly-by-wire without a mechanical back-up. The first digital system for a production application was not to take shape until 1978, when a digital quadruplex system with mechanical back-up was chosen for the F/A-18 Hornet.

The work of many companies, the flight-control system includes a triplex command stability augmentation system (Marconi Avionics/Bodenseewerk), an autopilot and flight director system (Marconi Avionics/Aeritalia), an air data set (Microtecnica), and a standby attitude and heading reference system (Litef).

The autopilot and flight-director system (AFDS) provides automatic flight control of the aircraft. Operating modes are as follows

Attitude and heading hold
Heading acquire
Track acquire
Altitude hold
Mach hold
Radar height hold
Terrain following
Auto throttle
Approach

Signals from the autopilot are passed to two AFDS processors which carry out the necessary computations in order to create autopilot command signals for the command stability augmentation system, and flight director command signals for the attitude director indicator and for display in the HUD.

As a safety precaution, the autopilot and flight director system continuously monitors and compares attitude information from the inertial system with that from the secondary attitude and heading reference (SAHR). Should these differ by more than a pre-set amount, the autopilot will automatically disengage, and warning indications will be passed to the crew.

The command stability augmentation system (CSAS) handles the joystick or autopilot-derived commands transmitted to it by the autopilot and flight director system. The system consists of three sets of triplicated rate gyros and two computers. As its name suggests, the pitch computer handles pitch computations, while the lateral computer deals with yaw and roll. The system compares the current angular acceleration in each

Right: The wing-sweep selector (inboard), and flap/slat selector are located close to the throttles, enabling them to be operated with a minimum of hand movement. Just aft of these is the pilot's hand controller.

Fly-by-wire system

Tornado's fly-by-wire flight control system combines mechanical, hydraulic and electronic components linked by a triplex (three-channel) electrical signalling system. SPILS is fitted only on Tornado ADV.

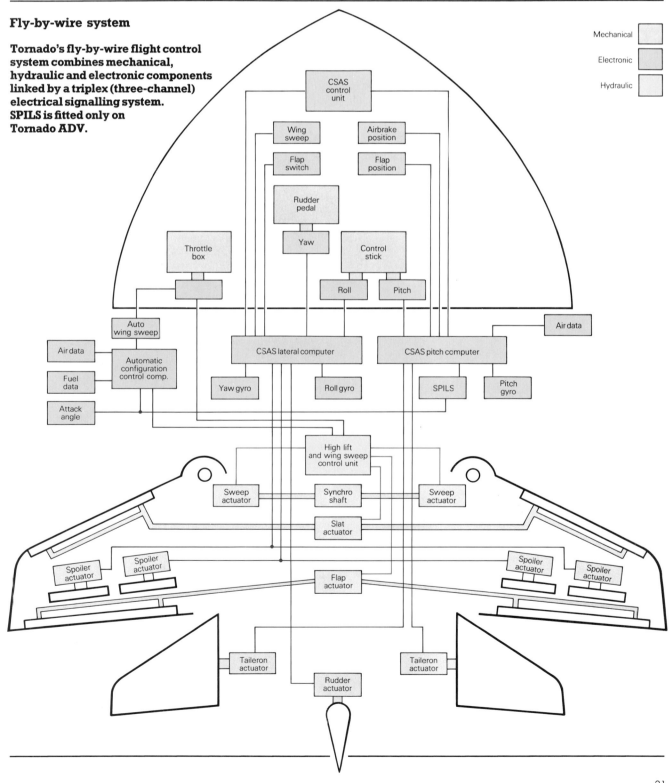

axis with the rate of turn being demanded. The latter may originate either from the pilot's controls or from the autopilot, both of which feed the manoeuvre/demand control loop. Any difference between the two results in an electrical correcting command, generated by the pitch or lateral computer and routed to the actuators of the appropriate control surfaces. In the process the CSAS takes account of aircraft speed and height data from the air-data computer, plus information on the current position of the wing sweep mechanism, airbrake, and spoilers to obtain the optimum control response.

Four basic angles of wing sweep are normally used: 25° at speeds of up to Mach 0.73, 45° up to Mach 0.88, 58° to Mach 0.9 and 67° at higher speeds. Flaps and slats are available only at 25°, slats alone at 45°, and at all greater angles slats and flaps are retracted.

The use of fly-by-wire does much to maintain the handling qualities of Tornado over a wide range of flight conditions. The system automatically compensates for the effect of gusts on the aircraft's flight path. Handling characteristics remain crisp, irrespective of flight conditions and the external load being carried. Between Mach 0.5 and 1.0, for example, the maximum roll rate remains constant at 0 to 4g not only for all altitudes and wing sweep positions, but also with all weapon loads. Full rudder may be used throughout the envelope, even at Mach 2. As a precaution against spins, the CSAS progressively reduces the available roll and yaw, enabling the pilot to manoeuvre freely without worrying about possible loss of control.

Processed terrain-following data from the radar's computer is passed to the aircraft's main computer, where it is integrated with that from the other navigational sensors. The resulting terrain-following commands are sent to the autopilot and the flying controls, or displayed in the pilot's HUD as flight-director demands for him to follow manually.

The CSAS incorporates a failure logic which continuously monitors the system, consolidating the triplicated signals which it is handling. A single failure creates no problems, but if multiple failures occur the normally declutched mechanical backup system will be engaged, allowing the aircraft to return to base.

Navigation system

High speed flight at low level poses severe navigational problems, since the crew and the aircraft's sensors cannot see very far ahead of the aircraft, and the average time available for the acquisition and tracking of even the most distinct targets is often less than five seconds. A publicity film made in the 1970s to promote the BAe Rapier anti-aircraft missile system gives a good illustration of the problem. Taken from the nose of a low-flying Canberra light bomber (hardly a high-performance aircraft by today's standards), it gives spectacular views of the terrain being overflown. Unless briefed on what to look for, few viewers will be able to spot some half a dozen typical military targets positioned on or close to the flight path. The Rapier missile sites positioned to guard these are even less obvious.

Another BAe photo, taken by an RAF Harrier, illustrates the difficulty of

Right: To ease pilot workload, vital systems such as the head-up display, moving-map, terrain-following radar, E-scope display and radar-warning equipment are all located in the centre of the IDS forward cockpit instrument panel.

detecting small targets at low level; it shows a white-painted Rapier unit parked in an open field. Uncamouflaged, and sited in the middle of the field, this might seem the easiest of targets, but the aircraft concerned had made three passes within lethal range before spotting it and taking the photo.

Experience has shown that unless the navigational aids (navaids) of a low-flying strike fighter can position the aircraft accurately along its intended flight path, targets are unlikely to be detected. A cross-track error of around 2,000ft (600m) is enough to ensure that the target will be detected too late to permit a single pass attack, if not missed completely.

No single currently available navaid will give the required level of accuracy on a realistic tactical mission, although this situation may change in the future. In order to be assured of detecting its target, Tornado carries several com-

IDS pilot's cockpit

1 Engine start panel
2 Wing sweep lever
3 Throttles
4 Manoeuvre and airbrakes switch
5 Pilot's hand controller
6 Communication control system (CCS) control panel
7 Bomb release safety lock (BRSL) control panel
8 Blank
9 Wander lamp
10 Oxygen connection panel
11 Oxygen supply panel
12 Blank
13 Crash panel
14 V/UHF control panel
15 Command and stability augmentation system (CSAS) control panel
16 Autopilot and flight director (AFDS) control panel
17 Canopy jack release handle
18 Internal canopy jettison handle
19 Emergency flap switch
20 Emergency airbrake switch
21 Flaps lever
22 Anti dazzle lights switch
23 Taxi thrust selector
24 LP cocks selector switches
25 Lift dump indicator
26 Reverse thrust indicators and override switch
27 Arrester hook push button and indicator
28 Master armament safety switch
29 Pilot's weapon aiming mode selector (WAMS) switches
30 Lighting dimmer control
31 Attention getter
32 Late arm switch
33 Angle of attack (AOA) indicator
34 Accelerometer
35 Attention getter
36 Manoeuvre monitor warning lamp
37 IFF mode 4 warning indicator
38 Approach progress indicator
39 Reheat operating lights
40 Clock
41 Flight refuelling lights
42 Standby compass
43 Landing gear emergency lowering lever
44 External stores jettison control
45 Secondary control surfaces position indicator
46 Land/taxi lights switch
47 Servo altimeter
48 Vertical speed indicator
49 Combined speed indicator
50 Landing gear position indicator
51 Nose wheel steering mode selector indicator
52 Radar altimeter
53 Autopilot engage indicator
54 "B" risk indicator
55 E-scope radar repeater display (ESRRD)
56 Attitude direction indicator (ADI)
57 Head up display (HUD) control panel
58 Head up display
59 Engine fire extinguisher
60 Blank
61 Remote frequency/channel indicator
62 Blank
63 Engine rpm indicators
64 Fuel flow indicator
65 Engine speed indicator selector switch
66 Oxygen flow indicator
67 Hydraulic pressure gauges
68 Fuel quantity indicator and selector unit
69 Engine temperature indicators
70 Nozzle area indicators
71 Emergency power supply (EPS)
72 EPS system on light
73 Hydraulic pressurization switches
74 Hydraulic utilities test switches
75 Brake selector handle
76 Brake pressure triple indicator
77 Central warning panel (CWP)
78 Repeater projected map display (RPMD)
79 Horizontal situation indicator (HSI)
80 HSI mode switch panel 2
81 Weapon control panel 2
82 Rapid takeoff panel
83 Control stick grip
84 Rudder pedals
85 Rudder pedals adjustment handle
86 Landing gear selector lever
87 Landing gear override button
88 Krüger flaps indicator
89 Brakes test button
90 Three axes trim indicator
91 Blank
92 Tacan control panel
93 HUD camera control panel
94 Engine control panel
95 Air intake ramps control panel
96 Terrain following (TF) radar control panel
97 Internal lights control panel
98 Engine test panel
99 Blank
100 Lamps test panel
101 Blank
102 Emergency UHF control panel
103 Environmental control panel
104 IFF control panel
105 Fuel control panel
106 Micro-detonating cord (MDC) safety pin stowage
107 Seat safety pin stowage
108 Canopy safety pin stowage
109 EPS safety pin stowage
110 Seat lower/raise switch
111 External lights panel

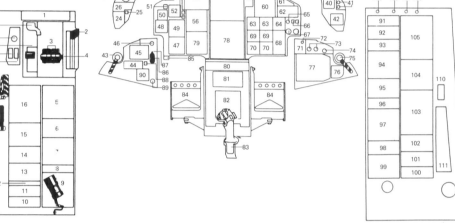

Right: The extent to which the Tornado IDS nav/attack system is computerized is emphasised by the dominance of the combined radar and projected map display and flanking CRTs with their associated keyboards in the rear cockpit.

plementary systems – an inertial platform, Doppler radar, and the secondary attitude and heading reference (SAHR).

The Ferranti FIN 1010 three-axis digital INS is the primary sensor for heading, attitude and velocity. Its vertical channel is mechanized to provide vertical velocity, and altitude using pressure-altitude data from the air-data computer. It may be aligned by any one of four methods – normal or rapid gyro-compassing, memorized heading or HUD alignment. Normal gyro-compassing takes 10-12 minutes and gives errors of less than 1nm/hr (1.8km/hr). The other three methods can be managed in two minutes, but result in higher errors.

The antenna for the Decca Type 72 Doppler radar is mounted beneath the fuselage of the aircraft, and illuminates the ground with four beams of energy. By measuring the Doppler shift in the reflected signal, the Type 72 is able to measure along-track and across-track velocity. Another navaid is the Marconi AD 2700 TACAN, a system also fitted to other British military aircraft such as the Harrier GR.3, Sea Harrier, Nimrod and Chinook.

Combining the output of these navaids into a single high-accuracy navigational fix requires a digital computer able to handle the complex mathematical calculations. Tornado was designed too early to incorporate the currently fashionable concept of distributed computing – the provision of localized computing power in any avionics unit which requires it (in this case the navigation system). Instead, the aircraft relies on a single computer which provides a centralized data-processing capability able to meet the demands of most sub-systems.

Known as the main computer, Litef's 16-bit Spirit 3 has 64K of memory. It stores, processes and distributes the data needed during the mission, handling information related to navigation, flight direction and terrain following, weapon aiming and delivery, and the EW systems.

Since the main items of Tornado avionics are digital, data is distributed around the aircraft in digital form. The system used reflects the technology of the early 1970s in that it requires a dedicated connection between a source of data and its destination. More recent aircraft use a digital highway to which all items of avionics are connected and along which the data may flow "addressed" to its destination. Normally designed to the standards of US Mil STD 1553B, such systems are due to find their way into later models of Tornado.

Cockpit displays

A large array of displays are needed to cope with the data from these systems. The pilot is equipped with a head-up display (HUD) of advanced design. This was developed by Smiths Industries in a programme shared with Teldix and OMI.

For head-down presentation of alphanumeric and graphical data, Elliott (later part of Marconi Avionics, now renamed GEC Avionics) developed multi-purpose cathode-ray tube (CRT) displays. In 1985 such a concept is commonplace; the text of this book first saw light of day on a CRT display attached to the author's personal computer, while combined graphics and text form part of many games played on inexpensive home computers. In 1971, however, such tech-

IDS navigator's cockpit

1 Blank
2 Mapping radar control panel
3 Head down display recorder (HDDR) control panel
4 Blank
5 Map stowage
6 Wander lamp
7 Blank
8 Oxygen connection panel
9 Oxygen supply panel
10 Blank
11 Blank
12 Blank
13 Canopy jack release handle
14 Internal canopy jettison handle
15 Attack release switch
16 Landing gear position indicator
17 Oxygen test button
18 Oxygen contents indicator
19 Oxygen flow indicators
20 Weapon control panel 1
21 Attention getter
22 Left CRT display
23 Altimeter
24 Combined speed indicator
25 Combined radar and projected map display (CRPMD)
26 Right CRT display
27 Attention getter
28 Blank
29 Accident data recorder (ADR) fail light
30 Central warning panel (CWP)
31 Blank
32 Blank
33 Blank

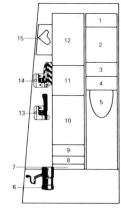
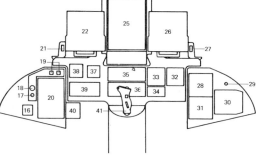

34 Blank
35 Navigation mode control panel
36 Weapon aiming mode selector (WAMS)
37 Artificial horizon
38 Blank
39 Blank
40 Clock
41 Navigator's hand controller

42 Cockpit voice recorder (CVR) control panel
43 Main computer (MC) control panel
44 Inertial navigator (IN) control panel
45 Secondary attitude and heading reference (SAHR) control panel
46 Internal lights panel
47 Blank
48 Blank
49 Blank
50 Blank
51 Blank
52 V/UHF control panel
53 Miscellaneous switch panel

54 Communication control system (CCS) control panel
55 Doppler control panel
56 Micro-detonating cord (MDC) safety pin stowage
57 Seat safety pin stowage
58 Command ejection selection lever
59 Seat lower/raise switch
60 Lamps test panel

nology was still uncommon outside laboratories, and the concept of applying it to an aircraft cockpit was a bold step forward in avionics design.

A new type of display required new terminology, and the new units were described as "TV tabulators" when the contract was awarded in 1971. This term was almost certainly the result of a slip of tongue or pen, but was widely adopted. "TV tabulator" eventually gave way to the more accurate "TV tabular display" or even "TV display unit". Current Panavia brochures simply refer to them as "CRT screens".

The object of all this technology is to present the pilot and the navigator with all the navigational and target data they will need, displaying it in a timely manner and in an easy-to-understand format. This sort of technology does not come cheaply – hence Tornado's high price tag – but it more than justifies the existence of the aircraft's elaborate avionics suite.

The latter has often been depicted by armchair critics of the programme as costly "black boxes" devised by a profligate electronics industry at the expense of the taxpayer in order to satisfy technology-hungry Air Marshals. The aircrew who fly Tornado take a very different view: the nav/attack system is what allows them to do their job while flying at the speeds and heights needed to give an adequate chance of survival in the face of SAM and anti-aircraft fire.

Before beginning a mission, the Tornado crew prepare a mission data tape. Recorded on a magnetic cassette, this contains details of waypoints, fixpoints (manmade or natural features to be used in obtaining navigational fixes), targets, and offset points (prominent features located close to targets not expected to show up well on radar). The completed tape is then loaded into the Tornado nav/attack system using the cockpit voice recorder. This accurately and rapidly inserts the data, but makes no allowance for last-minute changes in plan, which may be inserted manually using controls on the CRT display units.

Once alignment of the INS is complete, primary navigation mode is selected, feeding IN data to the aircraft's main computer. In normal operating mode the data from the INS and Doppler systems is passed to the main computer, where it is processed by a Kalman filter software routine. On its own, the best performance an INS can achieve is a drift rate of around 1nm (1.8km) per hour, but the Main Computer uses a statistical error model to provide an accurate estimate of position and velocity, with a drift rate less than one fourth that possible with pure INS.

If the FIN 1010 fails during the sortie, a secondary mode is automatically selected. This relies on data from the secondary attitude and heading system (SAHS) and the air data computer, and is one of three possible back-up modes which use different combinations of sensor, allowing the crew to cope with a sensor failure. A fourth and final back-up mode, provided in order to cope with a failure of the main computer, relies on the use of raw INS data.

Above: The rear cockpit of the trainer version of Tornado IDS (seen here in an uncompleted state, with some panels awaiting installation) is fitted with flying controls. Flight instruments replace the left-hand CRT display and the radar hand controller is moved to the right side console.

Navigation displays

Data is presented to the navigator via his displays. In addition to the CRTs, he has a combined radar and projected map display (CRPMD). Mounted between the CRT displays in the rear cockpit, this incorporates a computer-driven topographical map similar to those used in earlier types of moving-map display. The video image of the terrain ahead of the aircraft which is generated by the radar Ground Mapping modes may be superimposed on the moving map by means of an optical combiner system.

The navigator has several CRPMD display modes available, of which present position mode is likely to be the most commonly used. This places a marker (indicating the aircraft's current position) in the centre of the display, turning the map to match the aircraft's current track. The display may also be north-oriented, with the map being shown in the normal "north equals top" orientation, or ground-stabilized, with the map remaining stationary while the aircraft marker moves.

At the same time, alphanumeric and graphical data may be presented as required on the two multi-function CRT displays in the rear cockpit. Several

formats are available, the most common being PLN (plan), NAV (navigation) and F/A (fix/attack). Each is optimized for a different aspect of navigation.

Cinema films have made the wall map with ribbon-marked flight path used to brief World War II bomber crews part of aviation legend. An actor with a suitable stiff upper lip delivers the line "It's the Ruhr again tonight, chaps", the assembled aircrew groan their disapproval, and the wooden pointer is wielded to indicate the route, turning points, target and known areas of flak, while the navigators transfer the information to their own charts.

Tornado navigators don't need to scribble; such data is contained in the mission data tape which they have loaded into the nav/attack system, while their CRT displays can act as the modern equivalent of the 1940s wall map and ribbon. The PLN (plan) format gives the navigator a bird's eye view of the sortie, displaying the mission flight path in graphic form with north at the top of the screen and with a latitude and longitude grid superimposed. The flight path is displayed as a continuous line, with the waypoints identified by letters from the front end of the alphabet (A, B, D, and so on), and letters such as X, Y and Z marking target positions, while the aircraft's current position is indicated by a small circle. By using the keys below the screen the operator can change the scale of the display or call up additional information.

When NAV mode is selected the aircraft's position is depicted as a small circle in the centre of the screen. Use of a circle rather than a point results from the fact that the aircraft's position as deduced by the Kalman filter software routines in the Main Computer is, after all, only an estimate, and unlikely to be completely accurate. The system software is designed to draw a circle sized so that it has a 95 per cent probability of containing the true position.

A vertical line extending from the centre of the circle to the top of the screen and terminating in an arrow represents the current track of the aircraft. Directly above the arrowhead is a bearing scale which moves horizontally to create the CRT analogue of a compass. An outer circle used as a range marker carries the letter N somewhere on its circumference, marking the position of north. Two parallel lines indicate the cross-track error, while other symbology shows the next waypoint and the track to be flown from it. Alphanumeric data at the top left-hand corner of the screen shows the distance to the next waypoint and fixpoint, while characters in the upper right-hand corner show system time, TTG (time to go until the next waypoint is reached), and whether the aircraft will reach it early or late.

When approaching a navigational fixpoint or the target, F/A (fix/attack) mode is selected. Like PLN mode, this gives a highly simplified bird's eye view of the aircraft's position with respect to the fixpoint or target. The display is centred on the fixpoint, with the aircraft's track appearing as a vertical line. Superimposed on this track is a small circle marking the aircraft's current position, and preceded by two diverging lines which form a V-shape with the aircraft position marker at the apex. This latter feature indicates the limits of the radar horizontal scan. The alphanumeric data in the upper corners of the screen is the same as that displayed in NAV mode. Given such a graphic presentation of the run in to the fixpoint, it is easy for the navigator to compare this plan view with the radar image on the CRPMD. He is thus able to identify and mark the fixpoint or target within a few seconds.

If a target being attacked was not expected to show up prominently in the radar imagery, or if tactical circumstances or the local geography would make it undesirable or difficult to acquire, the mission data tape would have included up to three suitable offset points – radar-visible features in the vicinity of the target. One of these may be used for aiming without loss of accuracy while a one-button selector allows last-minute changes between offset and direct attacks and between blind or visual operation.

In addition to being marked on the navigator's CRPMD display, the target (or offset point) position is displayed in the field of view of the pilot's HUD. This marker is unlikely to coincide directly with the radar image on the CRPMD or the visual image seen through the HUD, since the marker position is derived from the aircraft's estimated position and thus includes any error in the latter. This error may be removed by aligning the marker with the target by means of a hand controller. This may be done by the pilot (using the HUD) or the navigator (using the radar image on the CRPMD).

Laser designation

Both crew members can also use the hand controllers to lock the radar or the chin-mounted laser ranger on to the target. Developed by Ferranti, this is the most accurate air-to-ground ranging device on the aircraft, and shares its housing with a marked-target seeker. In the early stages of the Tornado programme, plans existed for a retractable housing, but this was replaced by a fixed chisel fairing. The laser can be slaved to either the radar or the target marker in the HUD. Once aligned with the target it gives the Main Computer accurate three-dimensional co-ordinates, plus range and angle data, for use in weapon-release calculations.

If the target is being marked by an external laser designator, as might be the case if the aircraft were tasked with a close support mission, acquisition by the marked-target seeker will be automatic. The position of the target will then be indicated to the pilot via his HUD. If the autopilot is engaged, the target may be attacked without the pilot even seeing it.

Selection, arming and release of ordnance are handled by a Marconi Avionics/Selenia stores management system (SMS). This is a duplex system with two processors and two channels, each operating independently. Using a programming unit, the armourers load details of the weapon configuration into the SMS. Once the master armament switch has been set, the navigator can at any time programme up to three different attack "packages", specifying the type and number of weapon to be released, the intervals between the release of individual weapons, and the fuzing mode.

Once programmed, any of the three packages can be selected for release by pressing a single button. The SMS will then release the stores when commanded to do so by the Main Computer. In the event of a computer failure, it substitutes its own release cues based on the time intervals selected by the navigator. Selection of guns and infrared missiles is by the pilot's SMS panel.

The SMS incorporates an elaborate built-in test (BITE) system which is able to carry out the comprehensive pre-flight testing needed to make the carriage of live ordnance as safe as possible. Being software controlled, the system is flexible, and carriage of a new pattern of store can be dealt with by a software modification, always assuming that the weapon is compatible with the current pattern of ejector release units.

Straight-pass attack

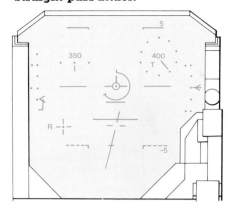

Above: HUD symbology during the final stage of a straight-pass attack includes a cross-shaped marker showing the predicted position of the target or a pre-selected offset point. This may be updated visually or by the radar or laser.

Unplanned targets

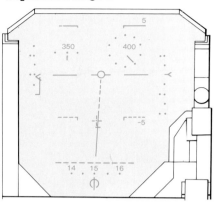

Above: When attacking a target of opportunity, the crew may select the Continuously Computed Impact Line (CCIL) display mode shown here. The near-vertical impact line seen in the centre of the HUD field of view must be laid over the target.

Air combat

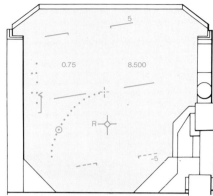

Above: If Tornado IDS is jumped by hostile fighters, or is tasked with a medium-range interception mission, the pilot can arm his guns and missiles and select the air combat HUD symbology shown above by pressing a single switch on the throttle.

Routine navigation

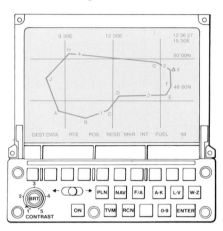

Above: The plan (PLN) format available on the CRT displays shows a map of the mission. Waypoints and targets are marked by letters from the front and back portions of the alphabet respectively, navigational fixpoints by numbers.

En-route navigation

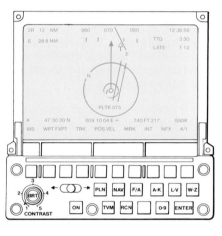

Above: The inner circle shows calculated aircraft position, while an 'N' on the outer circle indicates north. Current track (the vertical line) may be read against the scale at top centre, while the parallel lines show cross-track error.

Target ahead

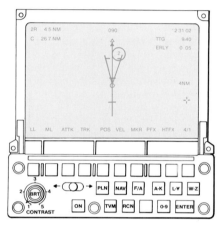

Above: For the final stages of the run in, the crew selects this target-centred Fix/Attack CRT mode. The small circle on the centre track line shows aircraft position and the vee-mark indicates radar scan limits, while the large circle marks the target.

Tornado IDS avionics suite

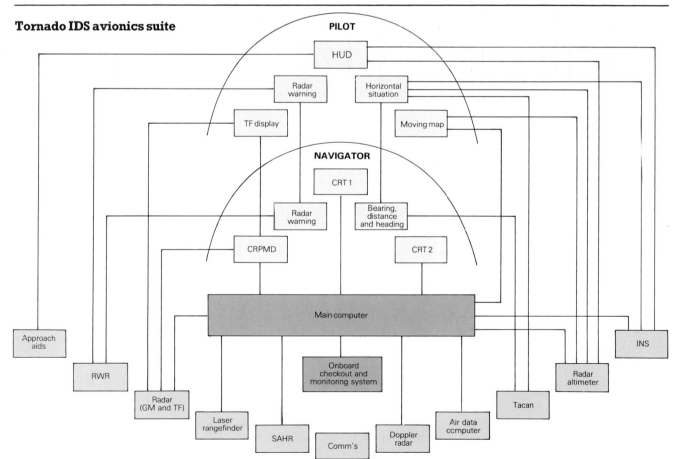

Above: This block diagram shows the main items in the avionics suite carried by Tornado IDS. This complex equipment allows the aircraft to fly pinpoint attacks at low level, but results in a high degree of complexity. All data transmission is digital, and most items of avionics feed data directly to the main computer, while others share data with the main computer and the pilot's or navigator's displays.

Several attack profiles can be flown, including a straight pass with retarded bombs or dispenser weapons, loft and dive attacks with bombs, stand-off attacks using air-to-surface missiles, or simple air-to-ground gunnery using the internally mounted cannon. The pilot takes aim by positioning the pipper over the target. Gun aiming calculations rely on slant range data from the ground mapping radar (used in air-to-ground ranging mode) or from the laser. This is used to position the pipper within the HUD field of view.

Not all Tornado's targets will be pre-planned and stored on the mission data tape: some will be targets of opportunity. If time permits, the pilot or navigator can use his hand controller to mark an unplanned target in the HUD or on the CRPMD. Once the nav/attack system has been informed about the new target, a normal automated attack sequence may be flown.

If time is short, as it probably will be, all forms of ordnance may also be delivered on targets of opportunity using CCIL (continuously-computed impact line) aiming and manual weapon release. During low-level flight CCIL aiming requires accurate height data with respect to the target; otherwise the ordnance will have a good chance of overshooting or falling short. Height above target will normally be obtained by combining range data from the laser with details of aircraft height obtained from the navigation system. Alternative solutions which may be used in the event of equipment failure involve obtaining data from the terrain-following radar, the radar altimeter or even a barometric altimeter.

Some unplanned targets will take the form of enemy interceptors, so an air-combat weapon aiming mode is also available for use against such targets or to enable Tornado to be used as a low/medium level interceptor. By pressing an air-to-air override switch on the throttle the pilot may cancel any previously selected weapon-aiming mode and prepare the aircraft for air combat, projecting the appropriate symbology into the HUD. Weapons available in air-to-air combat mode are the AIM-9 Sidewinder heat-seeking missile and the 27mm cannon (for air combat the latter are switched to a higher rate of fire) and three aiming modes are available – radar lock on, CCIL, and stadiametric ranging.

In addition to its offensive weapons Tornado carries an extensive electronic countermeasures (ECM) suite. This con-

Above: Twelve bombs form the offensive warload of this combat-ready Tornado IDS. Cerberus jammer (starboard) and BOZ 100 chaff/flare (port) ECM pods are carried on the outboard wing pylons.

sists of a radar warning receiver (RWR), a dispenser for chaff and flares and active ECM equipment designed to jam threat systems. As is generally the case with non-US electronic warfare systems, very little information is available on these items of equipment.

Electronic warfare systems
Aircraft of all three user nations are fitted with a radar-warning receiver (RWR), the antennas for which are mounted in a fairing near the top of the vertical fin, but there is no standard RWR, each nation having adopted its own solution. Germany adopted an RWR developed by Itek, which collaborated with AEG-Telefunken to modify the system for use on Tornado, while Italy selected equipment developed by Elettronica. Batch 1 and 2 aircraft delivered to the RAF carry an RWR developed by Elettronica, Marconi Space and Defence Systems, and AEG-Telefunken. Aircraft from Batch 3 onward have a new pattern of receiver, which has been developed by Marconi Defence Systems. Tornado GR.1 aircraft will be retrofitted with the ARI 18241/1 radar homing and warning receiver, an equipment developed for the ADV and described later in this chapter. It is not clear whether this will replace the tri-national system or all current patterns of RWR carried by RAF IDS aircraft.

The simplest countermeasure to radar and IR-guided threats is the use of chaff and decoy flares. To equip their Tornado fleets, Germany and the UK turned to Sweden's Philips Elektronikindustrier, adopting that company's BO series pod-mounted dispenser. Originally developed as the BOX 9 for Swedish Air Force use, this microprocessor-controlled pod was adopted by the French Air Force for use on Jaguar. The designation BOZ 100 has been reported for Luftwaffe and Navy pods, BOZ 107 for the RAF model.

Tornado is also equipped with active jamming systems, each nation having selected its own. British aircraft carry the

Right: This thermal image was created by a BAe Linescan 401 unit. Able to function by day or night, IR imagers are more useful for many tasks than conventional cameras.

Marconi Space and Defence Systems Sky Shadow, a pod-mounted jamming system which the service claims is the most advanced self-protection ECM pod in the Western world. Capable of operating in noise or deception modes, and disrupting pulse or CW radars, Sky Shadow is around 11ft 6in (3.35m) long and weighs more than 440lb (200kg). Designed for unlimited use even in high-speed low-altitude flight, it can automatically detect and identify threats using built-in receivers. Having assigned a priority to these threats, it can then deploy its transmitters against them, selecting the optimum frequency and modulation method.

The receivers are also used to "look-through" the jamming signals in order to assess the effect these are having on the hostile systems. If the threats under attack show no sign of being disrupted,

Sky Shadow can automatically change the type of jamming being used, repeating the exercise if necessary until the best result is obtained. Being software controlled, it can be re-programmed to cope with advances in enemy equipment and tactics.

Luftwaffe aircraft have in the past carried the Westinghouse ALQ-101 ECM pod, but for Tornado AEG-Telefunken has developed the Cerberus jamming system. This pod-mounted equipment is a multi-mode noise and deception jammer. Few details have been made public, but the pod is reported to have completed trials and to have entered production in 1985.

By the spring of 1985 the Italian Air Force had yet to select an EW system for its Tornado fleet. The service has traditionally preferred internally mounted EW suites supplied by Elettronica, and

MBB has devised this neat reconnaissance pod for German and Italian Tornado units. Carried on the aircraft centreline, it houses wide-angle cameras and an infra-red linescan unit.

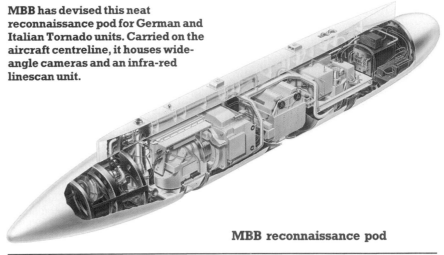

MBB reconnaissance pod

an internally mounted system designated EL-73 was reported to be under development by AEG-Telefunken and Elettronica in the late 1970s, but the Italian Air Force is now thought likely to select the Selenia ALQ-234 jamming pod. This self-defence pod uses noise and deception jamming techniques, and is designed for use against ground based threats operating in H, I and J band. A jammer designed to cope with Doppler and CW radars is mounted in the front section of the pod; behind this are two noise jammers, while the rear section houses the RWR and signal processing facilities used for power management of the system.

Other systems

The communications system mounted in the aircraft allows HF, UHF and VHF communications with the ground and with other aircraft. Some national variations exist in this area, with British and Italian aircraft carrying Plessey VHF/UHF radios, while Germany favoured Rohde & Schwarz. The latter company also supplied the HF single-sideband radios for German and British aircraft, while Italy adopted a Montedel set.

An IFF transponder is also carried. This unit is designed to respond to interrogation signals transmitted by surface or airborne radars, replying with a pre-arranged code which will identify the aircraft as "friendly". The status of NATO IFF systems is discussed later in this chapter when the avionics fit of the Tornado ADV is described.

Other specialized items of avionics are used for terminal navigation. The horizontal situation indicator (HSI) displays data from the tactical air navigation (Tacan) system, the UHF homing system (used for steering toward a ground or airborne signal source such as an airborne tanker), and the ILS (instrument landing system). Once the ILS receives the localizer and glideslope transmissions from the destination airfield, the pilot may choose to fly the aircraft manually, following the commands shown on the HSI, or to engage autopilot approach mode then monitor the subsequent flight path using the HUD.

All major items of avionics are packaged in the form of line-replaceable units (LRUs) which incorporate built-in test equipment (BITE) offering a high degree of self-test and status-monitoring capability. Since all major systems have facilities for either crew-initiated or continuous self-checking, the aircraft is ideally suited to operation from dispersed bases equipped with little more than supplies of fuel and ammunition.

Avionics LRUs are located in easily accessible bays which are cooled by air from the aircraft's environmental system, supplemented where necessary by cooling fans. The status of each LRU is indicated to the ground crew by means of a central maintenance panel mounted in the lower fuselage, and the replacement of faulty units requires only a few minutes' work – a simple matter of extracting the defective unit and inserting a replacement. No special tools are needed.

Specialized sensors have been devised for the reconnaissance role, and the German and Italian Air Forces rely on an external pod developed by MBB. Carried on the aircraft centreline, this houses two wide-angle cameras, an infra-red line scanner and the necessary support and data-storage facilities. Beyond taking up a hardpoint, the pod does not affect the aircraft's ability to carry ordnance or external fuel tanks, enabling the aircraft to be used for armed reconnaissance missions.

Linescan systems are widely used for reconnaissance purposes. These in-

volve an infra-red sensor scanning a narrow strip of terrain on either side of the aircraft's line of flight: as a result of aircraft motion, successive sweeps of the scanning head take in adjacent strips of terrain, building up a thermal image in the same way that the sequentially-scanned lines on a TV screen build up a visual image. The resulting imagery may be viewed in near real time by the navigator, allowing him to make a "quick-look" assessment of the success of the mission.

The Royal Air Force does not use the MBB pod, but in the short term relies on an internal equipment pack which can be fitted within the gun bays. This carries three IR linescan units – a single wide-angle scanner plus two sideways looking high definition scanners covering a complete 180° sector from one horizon to the other. A customized internal installation planned for future use is described in a later chapter.

ADV amendments

The interceptor role of the ADV has required significant changes to the avionics suite, with some items either modified or replaced and others not applicable to the ADV mission deleted. Biggest change is the replacement of the Texas Instruments terrain-following/ground mapping set by the Marconi Avionics AI24. The latter is often referred to as Foxhunter, a title which the RAF did not support but one which seems to have stuck.

Other new items of equipment on the ADV include a new Smiths Industries HUD, a Smiths Industries/Computing Devices missile-management system

and a second Ferranti FIN 1010 three-axis digital inertial platform (in Tornado IDS the back-up to the main FIN 1010 is a Decca Type 72 doppler radar), plus a Ferranti FH 31A horizon gyro in the rear cockpit. The latter unit is AC driven, and provides an attitude display for the navigator, plus pitch and roll systems needed by other items of avionics.

Existing equipment modified for use on the ADV includes the autopilot, the triplex command stability augmentation system and the Litef 16-bit computer. Memory size of the last is increased from 32K to 64K, with a further upgrading to 128K planned for the future. Virtually all computer software had to be rewritten – only the maintenance diagnostic routines could be directly adapted for use on the ADV.

The flight-control system is much improved. Tornado IDS aircrew must control the wing sweep, slats and flaps manually, whereas on the ADV wing sweep and flap/slat position are varied automatically by the flight-control system to match aircraft angle of attack. Another new feature is SPILS (spin and incidence limiting system), a two-channel system using analogue electronics.

The most important new feature is the AI24, a Marconi Avionics I-band (3cm) coherent multi-mode radar developed to meet a demanding Royal Air Force specification. AI24 was required to have a maximum range of more than 100nm (185km) against fighter targets, even if these were flying at low level, and a minimum range of around 300ft (100m) for the visual identification of targets in peacetime. Predicted target profiles include mass attacks by intruders flying

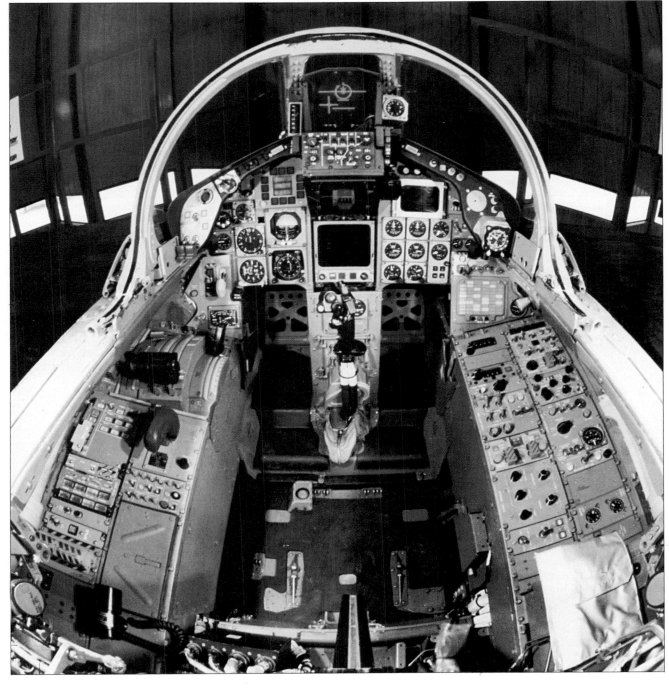

Above: Like the front office of the IDS, the pilot's cockpit of the Tornado ADV has been designed for ease of use, with centrally located displays and weapon-control panel.

at Mach 2.5 at 60,000ft (18,000m) or operating at low level under terrain-following radar control.

AI24 can operate either as part of a fully integrated ground- or AEW-controlled air defence system or autonomously if such a system were to break down under the stress of combat. The set is designed to cope with intense and sophisticated jamming, the designers having tried to anticipate tactics and ECM techniques likely to be used throughout the radar's operational life.

Initial flight tests of the AI24 were carried out in Canberra and Buccaneer testbeds, and the radar flew in Tornado for the first time on June 17, 1981. By the summer of 1980 tests with an early model had been completed, indicating that the AI24 was likely to meet its specification, but problems were to appear, with the result that when deliveries of Tornado ADV began in 1985, most of the aircraft were not fitted with radar, carrying ballast in the nose instead. These radar problems are not expected to delay the aircraft's entry into operational service, but early production aircraft will have a reduced-standard radar which is to be upgraded later.

The nose-mounted radar assembly consists of 12 liquid-cooled line-replaceable units (LRUs) positioned around a central transmitter assembly. Valves fitted to each LRU interface prevent coolant leakage as LRUs are withdrawn for servicing. Extensive use is made of lightweight materials such as magnesium (for cast components), plated aluminium (cables and wave-guides), and honeycomb and composites (structural components). Several of the LRUs contain microprocessors, which are used for data and signal processing.

The front end of the set is largely analogue, and consists of a coherent travelling-wave-tube (TWT) transmitter able to produce high mean levels of power over a wide bandwidth, an antenna of conventional Cassegrain configuration, and a low-noise receiver. The set also incorporates a J-band illuminator designed for use with the Sky Flash missile.

The use of a twist-reflecting Cassegrain antenna rather than a planar array of the type used in many US fighter radars is not due to technological conservatism. Conventional antennas still have advantages in applications where performance must remain consistent over a wide range of frequencies and sidelobes must be minimized. Dipole antennas for the IFF system are mounted on the surface of the main reflector, so are not normally visible. The antenna is light in weight, permitting the hydraulic scanning mechanism to provide agile slewing and accurate tracking over a wide range of angles.

Like the transmitter and antenna, the receiver is designed to operate over a wide bandwidth. It consists of an RF amplifier, followed by receiving and mixing circuitry. To provide good look-down performance and ECM resistance the receiver was designed to be able to handle low signal levels and high clutter returns without intermodulation distortion (the creation of spurious signals as a result of the mixing of two or more genuine signals).

The remainder of the AI24 is digital. Signals are passed initially to a frequency analyzer, which produces a series of spectra containing lines corresponding to all the received signals. This data is then passed to a high-speed processor known as the correlator, which identifies the wanted signals – those from real targets – and rejects returns from clutter, jamming or other forms of interference. By measuring the exact frequency of target signals the correlator is able to derive range and velocity data. These are passed to the radar data processor, which maintains track files on targets of interest, labelling and displaying them in the form required by the aircrew.

Like all modern radars, the AI24 presents data to the user in the form of synthetically generated symbology. The Weapon System Operator (WSO) has two CRT displays which offer a total of 15 display formats, all selectable (along with other parameters) by means of keyboards and conventional switches.

Target acquisition

The long-range search for targets will probably be carried out in pulse-Doppler mode, using a high PRF to maximize detection range. In this mode the set is able to discriminate between low-flying targets and ground or sea clutter. Initial display of targets will usually be on a range-versus-azimuth plot, with data on target bearing, range, elevation and radial velocity (known as range rate) being available.

At long ranges individual pulses will not have time to complete the trip out to the target and back to the radar before the next is transmitted, so target range is measured using frequency-modulated interrupted continuous wave (FMICW) techniques. By modulating the signal before transmission, then measuring the

Target search and acquisition

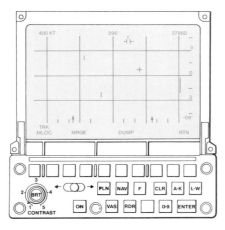

Above: This range versus azimuth search pattern is normally displayed on a CRT during combat air patrol. Targets appear as short vertical lines, IFF "friendlies" as crosses. The movable marker seen below one target is used for target selection.

Track While Scan

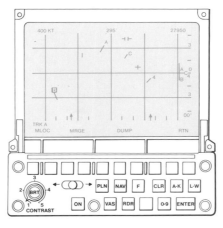

Above: With the AI24 radar set to track-while-scan mode, each hostile target is assigned a letter of the alphabet; other friendly aircraft taking part in the engagement are assigned numbers. "B" is a target outside the radar scan pattern.

Tactical Evaluation Display

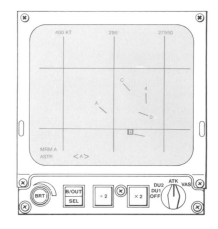

Above: Either crew member in the Tornado ADV may select the Tactical Evaluation Display (TED) for presentation on a CRT. This shows a plan view of all the targets being tracked. Target data may come from the AI24 radar, RHAWR or data link.

Skyflash attack CRT display

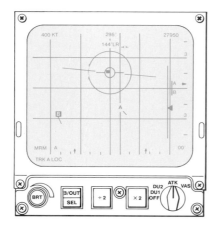

Above: "TRK A LOCKED" says the pilot's CRT display, while "MRM A" indicates that an attack is being made with Skyflash. The square solid aiming marker must be held within the large Allowable Steering Error circle during a collision-course attack.

Missile launch

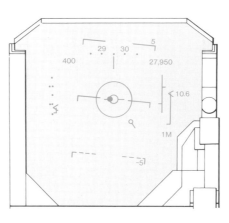

Above: The CRT symbology is duplicated in the HUD, along with vertical bar displays at the right hand side of the field of view. These show the missile launch zone (max/min launch ranges), with the triangle showing range to target.

Flight planning and navigation

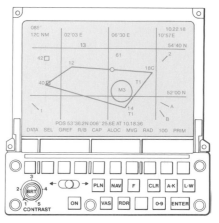

Above: Like the Tornado IDS, the ADV has a CRT mode able to display the sortie in plan form, with target tracks superimposed if necessary. By defining some points in vector form, the aircraft can automatically fly patrols over moving friendly forces.

exact frequency at the time of reception, the returned pulses can be identified and range calculated. Range resolution may be selected by varying the modulation pattern.

In tail-chase engagements the closing rate may be low, resulting in negligible Doppler shift from the target. To cope with such conditions AI24 also has low-PRF and pulse-compression modulations. Although the set was designed purely for air-interception duties, it does have a limited degree of ground-mapping capability when used in low-PRF mode. Beam-sharpening facilities are not available in pulse modes, however.

Targets of interest may then be monitored using FMICW track-while-scan (TWS) mode, the system maintaining track files in the main computer, and since the set continues to scan normally the target will have no way of telling that it has been singled out for attention. The number of targets which may be tracked simultaneously while the radar continues to search for other targets has never been revealed, but is at least 12, perhaps as many as 20.

Each target track is displayed on the TED, which gives a plan view of the tactical area. Individual tracks are labelled either with a number (for friendly targets) or a letter of the alphabet (if hostile), with the length and direction of the displayed vector indicating target groundspeed and relative track, and if additional data such as

heading, velocity or height is required the WSO can call this up in alphanumeric form. Target information passed to the aircraft via the data link is automatically correlated with the AI24 radar and IFF plots and tracks, and displayed to the crew within six seconds.

The ability to discriminate between hostile and friendly aircraft at long range is essential if the Sky Flash missiles are to be used to best advantage. This is a long-standing problem, and one which the West is attempting to solve. Without a successful solution, NATO's interceptors will be unable to deal with the large numbers of attackers that the Warsaw Pact might deploy in the event of a war on the Central Fronnt in Europe.

The most obvious answer is the use of IFF (Identification Friend or Foe) equipment. The IFF system selected for the Tornado ADV is the Cossor Electronics IFF 3500 airborne interrogator, also carried by RAF Phantom and Nimrod AEW aircraft and by Royal Navy Sea King helicopters. In the longer term this will be replaced by the planned NATO Identification System.

The IFF 3500 is designed to operate with the current NATO IFF system. Known as the Mk 10/12, it first entered service as the Mk 10 back in 1952 and no longer meets present-day requirements, having been considered obsolescent since the early 1970s. Many of the system's problems remain classified, since full knowledge of the details could

help an enemy to deceive or even exploit the system. (During World War II, the Luftwaffe learned how to interrogate the IFF system fitted to RAF bombers, and equipped its night fighter force with a homing system able to exploit the reply transmitted by the equipment in the bombers.)

Most problems stem from the relatively low operating frequency. The Mk 10/12 operates at the lower end of the frequency range used for radar – it transmits at 1,030MHz, and the aircraft-mounted beacons reply at 1,090MHz. Reflections from terrain or water prove more troublesome at these low frequencies than at radar frequencies, so the IFF system cannot interrogate low-flying targets at long range.

Another problem is that the low operating frequency gives the IFF antenna a much lower angular resolution than that of the radar on which it is mounted. Should a friendly aircraft be flying within the beam of the IFF antenna but outside the narrow beam of the radar, attempts to interrogate an unknown aircraft positioned within the main radar beam will result in the friendly aircraft receiving the interrogation signal and replying. To the radar operator, it will seem as if the unknown has replied as friendly.

The weaknesses of IFF, and the risk that it could be "spoofed" or exploited, have inspired efforts to find an alternative system able to identify targets. This subject is highly classified, but the

Combat Identification Technology programme being run by the Aeronautical Systems Division of the USAF Avionics Laboratory at Wright-Patterson AFB, Ohio, involves work in the fields of radar, electro-optics, lasers, and even space-based platforms.

Techniques for using radar warning receiver information to establish multiple target tracks and identifications have been explored by a US project to develop Radar Warning Receiver/Fire Control Interface Software (RFIS), and similar work has been carried out in the UK. Tornado ADV carries the Marconi Defence Systems ARI 1841/4 radar homing and warning receiver (RHAWR).

In the past, RWRs have been able to determine only the approximate bearing of the threats detected, usually by observing the relative strength of the signals received by the various antennas which feed the equipment. These have often been arranged to cover four 90° quadrants around the aircraft. To take an example, a signal received strongly by the forward facing antenna, less strongly by the starboard facing antenna, weakly by the port-facing antenna, and very weakly by the aft facing antenna, may be assumed to be coming from an emitter forward and to the right of the aircraft's flight path.

RWR signal analysis

For the ARI 1841/4, Marconi engineers decided to fit the sampling antennas in the vertical fin and the leading edges of the fixed inner wing section, and to measure not the strength of the signals from the individual antennas but their electrical phase. From these measurements it is possible to calculate the relative time at which the signal arrived at each antenna and thus accurately determine the bearing of the emitter.

This technique gives good results even at low frequencies, so the backseater is able to correlate intercepted signals with targets detected by the AI24. It will probably be possible to shut down the set for brief periods and track the targets by their radar emissions. In some cases the RWR may give the first alarm of an approaching target.

Another US project known as Multi-Source Integration (MSI) has investigated the feasibility of integrating data from cooperative systems such as IFF with information gleaned from other types of active and passive sensor on board a fighter. One possible source of target-identification data involves using sophisticated types of radar signal processing to study the characteristics of the radar echo. Research has shown that the signal reflected from a radar target is modified by the shape of that target. The ability to interpret such identity clues will be a characteristic of future fighter radars (including the new radar planned for the US Navy's F-14D version of Tomcat), and it is possible that a limited degree of target-identification capability has been incorporated into AI24.

One planned long-range sensor not present on early production aircraft is the GEC Avionics (formerly Marconi Avionics) electro-optical viewing system for long-range target identification, though the RAF is understood still to have a requirement for a long-range sensor of this type. Under initial plans the unit would have been located in a retractable mounting just ahead of the canopy, but no aircraft has been fitted with it. (The optical window mounted on the front surface of the ESM fairing during prototype trials was for a camera used to record missile launches.)

Having identified their target, the crew can then begin the attack, and if several targets are present the crew must decide the order in which they

Above: In the ADV trainer, a control column replaces the radar hand controller, while flight instruments displace the left-hand CRT display.

Left: The rear-cockpit Weapon Control Panel is used to select and monitor the armament. The pilot has a smaller unit of similar function.

should be attacked. The choice of the target to be attacked first should maximize the number which can subsequently be engaged, reducing the amount of time and fuel needed to switch from one to the next.

Tornado ADV has facilities for automatic target sequencing. The crew nominate up to four targets which they wish to attack, then specify tactical factors such as the type of missile to be fired and whether or not the afterburner is to be used. The computer examines all possible intercept sequences and indicates to the crew the attack pattern which will allow all targets to be engaged in the minimum overall time, taking into account factors such as the time needed to turn on to the different headings and climb or descend to the heights involved. Should this solution be unacceptable to the crew for any reason, pressing of a key will cause the system to display the alternative solutions in order of increasing intercept time.

Another aid to attack planning is LANCE (Line Algorithm of Navigation in a Combat Environment), which provides the crew with a combined tactical situation display and an indication of intercept steering. The first and second targets in an attack sequence are shown

in vector form, the ends of the target vectors indicating target position at the time of the longest practical missile interception. LANCE does this by calculating the maximum range of the missile under the prevailing tactical situation – the position at which the missile speed will have fallen off to that of the launch aircraft – and the time when this will occur. When the end of a LANCE vector coincides with the end of a target vector, the system gives an indication of the time of launch for a maximum-range kill.

If a long-range missile engagement is attempted, the WSO will probably switch to a velocity-versus-azimuth display in which each target is indicated by a triplet – three short vertical lines whose

spacing is proportional to target range. Once the radar is locked on to the target, allowable steering error is indicated by the position of a dot with respect to a circle: if the Tornado is flown to keep the dot within the circle, and the target is within the Sky Flash engagement zone, the attack should be successful. By returning the radar to scanning mode, another target may quickly be acquired.

The new HUD has a 20° field of view, and can display radar, visual identification, navigation flight-director and energy-management modes. A declutter mode reduces the information being presented to essentials only.

Two multi-function switches on the throttle allow the pilot to select an air-to-air override mode for visual combat at short range. A sequence of commands from these switches will set the radar and HUD to visual-combat mode, then select and prepare the missiles or gun. The radar will search in elevation over a restricted area, using a low PRF, automatically locking on to the nearest target. If the automatic scan pattern is insufficient to allow the AI24 or missile seekers to obtain lock-on, a hand controller located aft of the throttles can be used to slew the radar scanner or seeker heads until the target is detected.

Armament

The whole point of the exercise is to get the ordnance on the target. In addition to the normal range of bombs and guided weapons which arm most NATO aircraft, Tornado also carries a range of European-designed weaponry conceived with the Panavia warplane directly in mind, including the hard-hitting Mauser cannon. The one thing the aircraft currently lacks is stand-off weapons, which would remove the need to overfly tactical targets with consequent exposure to light SAMs and anti-aircraft artillery fire, but these are already being developed and will follow later in the aircraft's career.

If the motto of the British Royal Artillery is "Ubique" (Everywhere), the motto of Tornado ought to be "Omnia" (Everything). Its hardpoints can carry most types of tactical ordnance in the inventories of its users, including iron bombs, cluster munitions, napalm, air-to-air missiles such as the AIM-9 Sidewinder and Selenia Aspide and air-to-ground missiles ranging from the GBU-15 glide bomb and laser-guided Paveway to the TV-guided Maverick. In 1984, moreover, RAF Tornados were being fitted out to carry British tactical nuclear weapons: in an era of miniaturized thermonuclear weapons, it would be interesting to know just how big a nuclear punch the aircraft can carry.

Loadings used in action would depend on the operator and the mission, but the aircraft's avionics allow highly accurate attacks to be carried out even with conventional free-falling or retarded bombs. During early weapon trials bombs released at low altitude scored hits or near-misses against a 10ft (3m) diameter target, while toss-bombing attacks saw ordnance released against targets of similar size from points some 3-4 miles (5-6.5km) away impact within 30ft (9m) of the aiming point.

Tornado IDS also carries a pair of 27mm IWKA Mauser cannon, a high-velocity weapon of good accuracy. These are located side-by-side beneath the cabin floor, a common space being provided to collect the spent cases and links.

In addition to these basic weapons, Tornado will carry several types of weapon which have been specifically designed for it or for which it will be the principal delivery vehicle. Rather than describe at length the better-known weapons which Tornado carries, this chapter will concentrate on these more specialized items of ordnance.

MW-1 multipurpose dispenser

For attacks against ground targets such as air bases and AFV formations, Luftwaffe Tornados will be equipped with the sideways-firing MW-1 submunitions dispenser. Design work on this novel weapon started in 1966 when MBB was asked to meet a Luftwaffe requirement for a low-level strike weapon suitable for use against both Warsaw Pact airfields and the huge formations of tanks and other AFVs which would form the main thrust of any Warsaw Pact invasion of Western Europe.

The result was the Mehrzweckwaffe (multipurpose weapon), which consists of an aerodynamically shaped container carried beneath the fuselage of the aircraft. Assembled from four sections each containing 28 horizontally-mounted launch tubes, a single MW-1 has 112 tubes able to launch submunitions outwards to either side of the aircraft as it flies a low pass over the target. The launcher costs around DM100,000 – 10 per cent of the total cost of the loaded weapon – but re-use proved impractical:

once the submunitions have been released, the empty launcher will be jettisoned.

For anti-airfield strikes the MW-1 will carry a mix of three types of submunition. Destruction of runways and taxiways is handled by Stabo (Start-bahnbombe) cratering munitions to destroy the hard surface, while MIFF mines – a mixture of active and passive mines fitted with acoustic sensors – will complicate the task of damage repair. Hardened aircraft shelters and supply sites must also be destroyed, a task for specialized shelter bombs. According to Luftwaffe studies, a single MW-1 equipped Tornado should be able to knock out 16 aircraft shelters, while two aircraft should be able to neutralize a complete airfield.

Attacks against battlefield targets also involve three types of submunition, with MIFF mines backed up by KB-44 hollow-charge anti-tank bomblets and shrapnel bombs designed to cope with soft targets such as trucks. Each MW-1 launch tube can carry 42 KB-44s and eject them in only 0.6 seconds: according to the Luftwaffe, a single MW-1 fired against a formation of ten AFVs would knock out four of the target vehicles.

Initial trials were carried out using F-104G Starfighter test aircraft, then F-4F Phantoms. These identified problems with bomblet ejection, and the free-flight stability of the anti-tank bomblets, and transition from the F-4 to the Tornado also proved troublesome.

A pre-series production contract was given to MBB in January 1982, and development of the anti-armour version was the first to be completed. Working under a procurement-anticipation contract, MBB prepared for full production, and a contract for this was expected in 1985. Development of the anti-airfield version

Above: When tasked with anti-airfield or anti-armour missions, Luftwaffe Tornados will carry the MW-1, a sideways firing dispenser for specialized submunitions. Once the latter have been released the empty dispenser is jettisoned to reduce drag.

is due to be completed by the end of 1985, with first deliveries in 1987.

MW-1 has proved an expensive project. Total programme cost is likely to be around DM1.426 billion, with DM470 million having been spent on development, and DM941 million already allocated to production. Plans to procure 1,500 MW-1s for the Luftwaffe had to be scaled down to a total of 860, and further cutbacks could reduce this figure.

The US Air Force expressed an interest in MW-1, and has tested several versions. MW-1 could have proved a useful weapon for the Fairchild A-10A, but Congress not only denied $2 million requested in FY80 for further evaluation, but also ordered a cutback in funding already allocated. The result was the decision in FY81 to cancel the USAF trials programme.

In December 1984 the US and West Germany signed an MoU covering the joint evaluation of anti-airfield weapons and runway-repair techniques. During tests carried out at Eglin AFB, an MW-1-equipped Tornado was used to dispense Stabo submunitions against a runway target. US and German runway clearing and repair equipment and techniques were then used to repair the resulting damage. In parallel with this work, the US BLU-106B Boosted Kinetic Energy Penetrator (BKEP) submunition was evaluated at Germany's Meppen Weapon Test Range to test its effectiveness against hardened aircraft shelters.

Top: This target's eye view of the MW-1 dispenser in action shows the release of KB44 anti-tank bomblets. Each of the dispenser's 112 launch tubes can carry 42 bomblets and eject them in 0.6 seconds to create a dense pattern on the ground.

Sole export user of the MW-1 is likely to be Italy, which has studied a possible purchase of the anti-airfield version. Negotiations were under way in late 1985 on a Memorandum of Understanding under which the Italian Air Force would equip its Tornado fleet with an undisclosed number of MW-1 systems, and Italian industry would receive industrial offset work.

JP233 for airfield attack

MW-1 is expected to become operational at roughly the same time as the JP233, a British weapon intended to deny the Warsaw Pact unrestricted use of its airfields in wartime. Developed by Hunting Engineering, JP233 dispenses a mixture of specialized cratering and area denial munitions. Formerly known in the US as Low Altitude Airfield Attack System (LAAAS), it uses downward ejection, and is carried beneath the wing of the attacking aircraft. The weapon is made up of two sections, each of which houses a dispenser plus a payload of submunitions. Unlike the MW-1, it has no anti-armour capability: apart from airfields, the only targets against which it would prove effective are railway yards, road junctions and supply depots.

The payload consists of 30 SG 357 cratering submunitions, plus 215 HB 876 area denial submunitions. Both types are dispensed simultaneously, descending by parachute. The SG 357 is designed to penetrate and break up the hardened surface of runways and taxiways, while the HB 876 combines anti-personnel and anti-repair vehicle functions, hampering repair operations. A built-in timer will detonate HB 876 warheads at near-random intervals – a measure intended to discourage personnel from approaching. If struck by the blade of a bulldozer, the HB 876 is designed to tilt its main axis towards the impact before detonating with sufficient force to fire a high-velocity slug through the blade, knocking out the clearance vehicle.

JP233 started life as a UK national programme, with project definition studies beginning in 1975. While this work on the development of the dispenser and its submunitions was underway, the programme attracted significant USAF interest. In August 1976 the United States joined the project, in order to evaluate the weapon with a view to joining in full development.

The joint project-definition phase was followed by a validation phase which led to a US decision to join the programme in order to obtain a modern anti-airfield weapon for its F-111 fleet. Under a joint US/UK agreement, management of the JP233 programme remained the responsibility of the UK MoD, while a USAF system programme director was appointed associate and other US personnel supported the development work; costs were to be shared 50:50, and since the UK had already spent the equivalent of around $26 million on JP233, the US paid $11.3 million as its share of the costs to date.

Full-scale development started in October 1977, when work began on creating dispensers suitable for use on Tornado and the US aircraft, and the construction and test of dispenser systems continued through the late 1970s. The USAF planned to procure enough JP233 equipments for 1,828 sorties. Each F-111 would have carried four dispensers on underwing pylons – two with mines and two with cratering bomblets.

One problem which soon raised its head was the UK's high inflation rate, and the unstable relationship between the pound sterling and the US dollar. The estimated cost of the total programme jumped from $128.3 million in FY79 to $193.5 million in FY80, then $218 million in FY81. This ever-increasing bill raised the ire of the House Appropriations Committee of the US Congress, who voted to cancel all FY81 funding. The official reason for the cancellation was that the cost of the weapon had risen by more than 10 per cent in 1978 constant pounds, meeting the conditions of an escape clause written into the original US/UK agreement. The Committee suggested that alternative weapons such as the BAP-100 anti-runway bomb, CRV-7 rocket, and Durandal anti-runway dispenser be considered as alternatives for short-term use, and that development of a US anti-airfield weapon be started.

In February 1981 the General Accounting Office of the US Congress issued a report which strongly criticized the USAF's JP223 planning. The Service had failed to complete a mission analysis, the report claimed, and the escalating cost also attracted unfavourable comment.

Within weeks of the release of this document it seemed that the USAF might still be allowed to buy the British weapon. The new administration of President Reagan was apparently willing to foot the bill, requesting $66 million in FY81 and an additional $60 million over and above the $10 million which the outgoing Carter administration had proposed for FY82. By the end of the year, however, the programme was once again dropped, and the USAF was eventually to settle for the Matra Durandal.

Surprisingly for a nation renowned for defence dithering, the UK continued to back the programme on a national basis. Withdrawal of USAF support would increase the cost of the programme by only 10 per cent, it was announced. Initial production, ordered in 1983, was under way by the end of 1984, with JP233 due to enter service in late 1985 or early 1986, and the RAF expected to buy 500 systems by the end of the decade.

Working under prime contractor Hunting Engineering is an industrial team which spans the UK industry. ML Aviation is responsible for the runway cratering dispenser and special connectors, while Ferranti Instrumentation tackles the area denial submunition and dispenser. Most of the explosives-related work is handled by Royal Ordnance factories at Patricroft (warheads), Bridgewater (explosives), Blackburn (arming units) and Glascoed (filling and assembly of warheads). Thorn EMI handles some of the electronics, while Irvin GB supplies the retarding parachutes fitted to the runway-cratering munitions.

Kormoran anti-ship missile

Tornados in service with the Federal German Navy carry the MBB Kormoran anti-ship missile, a weapon designed in the late 1960s by Bölkow (now part of MBB) and Nord Aviation (itself now a part of Aérospatiale). Development was delayed by a series of problems, and a production contract was not signed until

Above: Tornado ZA354 prepares to test two JP223 anti-airfield weapons.

Right: Having released its full load of submunitions, the aircraft offers a close-up view of the dispensers' empty compartments.

Below: Submunitions tumble from a JP233's tandem dispensers. The large SG 357s from the rear section are designed to break up the surface of runways and taxiways, while the smaller HB 876 area-denial mines will hinder repair work.

1976. In September of the following year four missiles were successfully fired, meeting a German MoD acceptance condition for the weapon, and the first production missiles were delivered three months later, entering service on German Navy F-104G Starfighters.

Delivery of 350 missiles to the Marineflieger has been completed, and a batch of 60 destined for use on Italian Navy Tornados is under construction. Without further orders the line would have to close in the mid-1980s, since the planned Kormoran 2 follow-on will not be ready for production until the late 1980s. Brazil or Italy might order missiles to arm their subsonic AM-X strike fighters.

In combat, Tornado's crew will lock the radar of their aircraft on to the target, then pass the resulting target co-ordinates to the aircraft-mounted missile computer for loading into the missile. If hostile jamming or the effects of bad weather prevent radar lock on, the crew will use a small joystick to position a marker over the target image on the cockpit CRT display. If jamming is so intense that even this is impossible, or if the radar fails during the mission, the Tornado may be flown to within visual range of the target where it can be picked up in the aircraft's optical sight.

Kormoran has a two-stage propulsion system. Immediately after launch, two solid-propellent boosters accelerate the weapon to its high subsonic cruise speed; the remainder of the flight is under the power of a solid propellant sustainer motor with a burn time of 100 seconds.

Most of the flight to the target is under the control of the missile's inertial guidance system, and much of it takes place at around 65ft (20m) above the water, descending to between 6.5 and 17ft (2-5m) for the final attack. After flying a predetermined distance the missile energizes its active-radar seeker, which scans a search pattern until a target is detected. After lock-on, the round flies the rest of the way in radar-homing mode.

A delay fuze allows the missile to penetrate the target ship before detonating the 1,220lb (56kg) explosive charge deep within it. Two rows of projectile charges positioned in two rows around the outer casing of the warhead are ejected outward at high speed. Able to penetrate between 2.75-3.5in (70-90mm) of steel, they easily deal with bulkheads inside the target ship, spreading the damage into other compartments of the vessel.

Sea Eagle potential

Standard long-range anti-ship missile of the Royal Air Force is the BAe Sea Eagle, originally known as P3T and based on the aerodynamic design of the earlier Anglo-French Martel. Development firings began in 1981, and were virtually complete by early 1985, with service entry later that year.

The UK has no immediate plans to install Sea Eagle on RAF Tornados. In the short-term, instead, the missile will be carried by Hawker Siddeley Buccaneer light bombers assigned to the maritime-strike role, and by BAe Sea Harrier fighters. The surviving Buccaneers are being upgraded, so presumably have a reasonable service life ahead of them, but when they finally retire their anti-shipping role – and Sea Eagle missiles – will probably be inherited by Tornado.

Sea Eagle can be interfaced easily with any aircraft equipped with a digital weapon-management system, so its deployment on Tornado should be a simple matter, and models of Sea Eagle-armed Tornados have been exhibited by BAe. Analogue-to-digital converters and a simple weapon-control panel

Above: 98+05 in Marineflieger markings shows off the Kormoran missiles that German Navy and Italian Air Force Tornados will carry for anti-shipping strikes.

Below: Like many types of anti-ship missile, Kormoran is designed to make its final approach at low level, entering the side of the target's hull for maximum effect.

allow Sea Eagle to be fitted to analogue aircraft such as Buccaneer.

Like Kormoran, the BAe missile must be supplied with target range and bearing data from the aircraft's nav/attack system. It also requires data such as launch airspeed, wind speed and direction, target-selection criteria and ECM information. If this information is not available due to jamming or equipment failure in the launch aircraft, Sea Eagle may be released on a pre-set heading and allowed to fly towards the target area until its own radar seeker detects and locks on to the target.

The general operating principle of Sea Eagle is similar to that of Kormoran, but the missile is powered by a small turbojet engine rather than rocket motors. For carriage on the pylon of the launch aircraft the air intake is covered, but after ejection the cover is jettisoned, allowing air to flow down the intake duct and into the engine and causing the rotating parts to windmill up to a speed at which the fuel may be turned on and the engine started.

The flight computer within the round then issues the instructions needed to make the weapon descend to sea-skimming height while simultaneously turning on to the target bearing. Attacks are

not limited to simple profiles. During flight tests, one round has demonstrated the ability to overfly the first target it detects and to hit a second, while two have been ripple-fired at the same target, making their approach from different directions. Maximum range has not been announced, but could be up to 60 miles (100km).

As the round nears the target area, the flight-control computer activates the radar seeker. This is a J-band active pulse-radar device whose large scan angle and long range are designed to ensure that even fast-moving and evasive targets will still be within the search area. In designing the seeker, Marconi ensured that it would be able to cope with the severest weather conditions. During trials it has detected targets with radar cross sections of 100m² or more, tracking them from the radar horizon to within a few hundred metres.

Once lock-on has been obtained, the round descends to a lower height for the final stage of its attack. On impact with the target vessel the destructive power of the high-explosive warhead is enhanced by the kinetic energy of the impact, and the ignition and dispersal of the residual fuel from the weapon's propulsion system. This should ensure

the incapacitation or destruction of most warships. In July 1984 a Sea Eagle round fitted with a live warhead was fired at the decommissioned Royal Navy County-class destroyer *Devonshire*. The missile badly damaged the target, BAe announced, adding that an operational vessel would have been completely deactivated by the effects of the strike.

Sky Flash for the ADV

For the first part of Tornado ADV's operational career, its long-range weapon will be the BAe Sky Flash, a medium-range, all-weather air-to-air missile using semi-active radar guidance. Development of Sky Flash dates back to 1972, when the UK decided to switch its Phantom fleet from the strike role to that of air defence. The SEPECAT Jaguar was coming into service to handle attack missions, allowing the US fighter to replace most of the older BAC Lightning fighters. The new role required a large stock of air-to-air missiles. Although the cheapest course would have been to purchase more AIM-7E Sparrows from the USA, the known limitations of this weapon – particularly its vulnerability to ECM – would have given it a short service life.

A study carried out by UK industry and the Royal Aircraft Establishment concluded that a suitable missile could be created at relatively low development cost by combining the proven airframe, warhead and rocket engine of the US AIM-7E Sparrow with two new systems already existing in experimental form – an advanced radar seeker developed by Marconi and an EMI proximity fuze. With an eventual eye to the planned Tornado ADV, the MoD decided to back the development of a Sparrow-based British missile using this technology to arm the Phantom interceptors in the late 1970s and early 1980s, and in an improved Mk 2 form to serve well into the 1990s on the Tornado ADV.

An Air Staff Requirement issued in January 1973 defined the performance characteristics of the new missile, calling for improvements over the AIM-7E in areas such as accuracy, fuzing reliability, resistance to ECM, discrimination between targets and clutter, and the ability to pick out a single target from a closely-spaced group of attackers. Development of what was then known by the designation XJ521 was ordered in December 1973.

The task was not just a simple matter of installing the new seeker and fuze into the US missile: BAe also developed new guidance and control systems including an autopilot, actuator systems and a power supply.

Test firings began in 1976 at US ranges such as Point Mugu, since these were already well-equipped to handle the F-4 and AIM-7, and the first five shots took place from a US Navy F-4J at Point Mugu. All were successful. By the time development firings ended in December 1978, 22 rounds had been launched, all but two either passing within lethal range of the target or scoring direct hits.

A further series of firings was then carried out by the USAF and US Navy, which wished to evaluate the missile. The US was becoming disenchanted with its home-grown improved Sparrow, the AIM-7F, but there was probably never any real desire to adopt XJ521, by then known as Sky Flash. Like Tornado, the British missile became the target for a knocking campaign: information leaked to selected US defence journalists assured them that the weapon had severe deficiencies, and that the British successes were due to the targets having been fitted with radar-augmentation systems designed to make them better targets.

The secret of successful disinformation is to mix truth with falsehood, and this was a classic example of such tactics. The targets had indeed been augmented to increase their effective radar target area, but this is an essential feature of any missile trial involving custom-built target drones. Being much smaller in physical size than manned aircraft, drones are unrealistically small targets, and augmentation is needed to bring their radar echoing area up to that of a manned aircraft.

Swedish assessment

A more realistic assessment of Sky Flash was that performed by the Royal Swedish Air Force, which needed a medium-range missile to arm the JA37 interceptor version of its Viggen fighter. All three "improved Sparrows" were evaluated – Sky Flash, AIM-7F and the Italian Aspide, another Sparrow-based round with all-new guidance and control systems. The Italian weapon was being designed on a later timescale than Sky Flash so could in theory use even more modern technology. The Swedes liked the idea, but unfortunately the Selenia weapon was being developed for surface-to-air applications, with air-to-air versions an option for the future. Faced with a realistic choice between AIM-7F and Sky Flash, Sweden chose the British missile in 1976.

In August 1979 the RAF carried out its first launch from a Phantom, bringing the career of a Meteor drone to an abrupt halt. The weapon entered RAF service in 1978. Modifications were needed to match the Phantom to its new weapon, but these were minor, reportedly costing around £1,000 per aircraft, and did not affect the ability to fire AIM-7E.

The first firing from a Viggen, in April 1979, resulted in the destruction of the target drone. In October 1980 production deliveries to the Swedish Air Force began, and the weapon is in service as the Rb.71. Sales to Sweden exceed £85 million, with further orders anticipated to arm the JAS39 Gripen, and by December 1983 BAe had delivered 1,000 pro-

duction rounds in two years. The RAF is thought to have a requirement for a total of around 2,500 missiles, and production could run until 1987 on current orders.

First release of Sky Flash from a Tornado ADV prototype took place in November 1981 when an inert missile was used to check the separation of the missile from the aircraft. Guided launch from Tornado did not begin until February 1985, but the first was immediately pronounced a success.

One problem with semi-flush mounted missiles is that the airflow around the fuselage tends to hold them in place. For the Tornado, Frazer-Nash has developed a launcher whose pyrotechnically actuated rams apply a force of up to 4 tons to the missile, forcing it away from the fuselage and through the airflow around the aircraft. According to the company, it is the first launcher able to achieve clean separation of missiles at any point in the launch aircraft flight envelope. Development of the launcher took longer than anticipated, but the production rate was able to match the pace of ADV deliveries.

Shortly after takeoff, the crew of Tornado will briefly activate the Sky Flash missiles in order to tune their guidance systems to the selected opera-

Above: The Tornado F.2 and F.3 are armed with BAe Dynamics Sky Flash missiles. Based on the proven Sparrow airframe and propulsion system, these are carried in Phantom-style semi-flush mountings in the fuselage underside.

Below: A Frazer-Nash launcher incorporating pyrotechnically actuated rams thrusts the Sky Flash missile away from the Tornado fuselage, ensuring a clean separation at all points in the aircraft's performance envelope.

ting frequency of the AI24's J-band radar illuminator. Pre-tuning the missiles in this way reduces reaction time on reactivation to around two or three seconds.

In order to assign a missile to a target which is being tracked by the AI24, details of the Doppler frequency-shift resulting from the target's velocity with respect to the launch aircraft must be fed to the seeker electronics. The seeker on the missile is steerable in elevation and azimuth, and can be pointed more than 40° from the missile centreline. During pre-launch operations it is slaved to the antenna of the AI24, so that it points towards the target which the radar is tracking. Missile control-system gains must also be set to match the conditions of the engagement. Adjustment for height is carried out automatically, but the pilot must manually select short- or medium-range control system gains.

When the firing button is pressed there is a delay of two or three seconds before the missile leaves the pylon while the round's thermal batteries are energized. Designed to provide the power needed by the various missile systems, these are one-shot devices which use a pyrotechnic charge to generate the necessary operating temperature.

Like the AIM-7E Sparrow, Sky Flash is a boost/coast weapon powered by a single-stage solid-propellent rocket motor. The missile accelerates to Mach 4 within five seconds, then coasts for the rest of the flight, its velocity gradually falling away. In the early stages of flight the warhead fuzing system is inhibited, a safety precaution designed to protect the launch aircraft. Maximum range is more than 40km and the missile can perform snap-up and snap-down attacks, coping with targets down to 250ft (75m).

The nose-mounted seeker is of the inverse-monopulse type, and tracks the target by observing the reflected energy from the J-band CW illuminator in the AI24 radar. A second antenna mounted on one of the missile fins is rear-facing, and is used to monitor the CW energy leaving the antenna of the AI24. This "raw" CW energy acts a reference signal, so that the seeker can measure the Doppler shift of the energy reflected from the target and thus deduce target velocity. This facility allows the seeker to distinguish between the target and land or sea clutter.

The BAe-designed autopilot translates steering commands from the seeker into movements of the missile's cruciform wings, one pair of which provides pitch control while the other controls roll. The tail fins are fixed. Sky Flash uses proportional navigation – lateral acceleration of the missile in flight is proportional to the missile/target sight-line rotation rate and to the missile-to-target closing speed – and is highly accurate. Exact figures are classified, but early flight tests demonstrated average miss distances of 4-7ft (1-2m).

As the round passes within lethal range of the target, the warhead is triggered by the radar proximity fuze, although contact fuzes are also fitted. The warhead is of the continuous-rod type, and weighs 66lb (30kg).

Tornado ADV was to have been armed with Sky Flash Mk 2, an improved missile with greater range and all-round coverage, better performance against manoeuvring targets, and improved ECM resistance. This was cancelled in January 1981 when the UK decided to adopt the Hughes AIM-120 AMRAAM (Advanced Medium Range Air-to-Air Missile), but some of its features have now been incorporated into the Mk 1. A new pattern of rocket motor under development incorporates a sustainer section which will improve performance against high-flying targets.

Short-range Sidewinder

At shorter ranges, the ADV can use the AIM-9L Sidewinder. At first, it was planned that these would be fitted to the outboard wing pylons, but by the time the first prototype was rolled out, a neat auxiliary launch rail able to fit on the side face of an underwing pylon had been devised. This allows the small heat-seeking missile to be carried with minimal drag penalty while leaving the hardpoint free to carry an external tank. On long-range ferry missions, the aircraft would not carry Sky Flash, but four tanks plus two Sidewinders.

Current US production models are the AIM-9M for the US Services and the -9P for export. Tornado ADV will carry the earlier AIM-9L, which is now being manufactured in Western Europe by a consortium headed by Bodenseewerk, and in Japan by Mitsubishi.

Although the US Navy plans to convert stocks of AIM-9L missiles to the improved -9M standard, the AIM-9L is likely to remain the standard Royal Air Force short-range missile until the planned AIM-132 ASRAAM (Advanced Air-to-Air Short Range Missile) enters service in the 1990s, but export customers may use other models of Sidewinder such as the AIM-9M or even the Matra Magic 2 or MICA.

The AIM-9M incorporates a seeker whose detector element is refrigerated by a closed-cycle cooler. The ability to discriminate between targets and the terrain background during low-level engagements is improved, as is resistance to countermeasures. A new rocket motor generates less smoke than the earlier patterns, reducing the missile's visual signature and giving the victim less warning of missile launch.

Having flown the cannonless F-4 Phantom, and been forced to restore guns to the BAC Lightning, the RAF was determined to have cannon armament on the ADV. The new fighter was too early in timescale to take advantage of the new British 25mm ADEN cannon, so the 27mm Mauser was retained. Studies of likely ADV operations suggested that for most missions a single cannon would provide an acceptable level of firepower, so the port-side cannon was deleted when the ADV fuselage was designed.

Two gunsight modes are available on the HUD. In primary mode, target range and velocity data from the radar is used to position an aiming reticle, while secondary mode involves the display of a "hot line" – a simulation of the theoretical path which the cannon projectiles will follow.

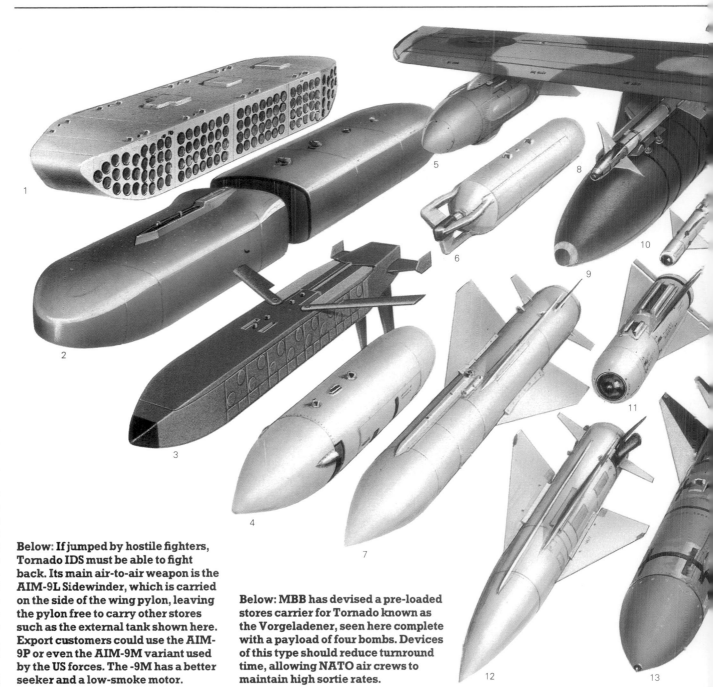

Below: If jumped by hostile fighters, Tornado IDS must be able to fight back. Its main air-to-air weapon is the AIM-9L Sidewinder, which is carried on the side of the wing pylon, leaving the pylon free to carry other stores such as the external tank shown here. Export customers could use the AIM-9P or even the AIM-9M variant used by the US forces. The -9M has a better seeker and a low-smoke motor.

Below: MBB has devised a pre-loaded stores carrier for Tornado known as the Vorgeladener, seen here complete with a payload of four bombs. Devices of this type should reduce turnround time, allowing NATO air crews to maintain high sortie rates.

Right: Several Tornado prototypes were used during armament trials. The aircraft shown here, XX947, is the third prototype and the first dual-control example. Loaded with a typical strike payload, it carries iron bombs under the fuselage, plus external tanks inboard and ECM pods outboard on swivelling wing pylons. Each operator has chosen its own jamming pod: Britain uses the Marconi Sky Shadow, Germany opted for the AEG-Telefunken Cerberus and Italy may adopt the Selenia ALQ-234.

Tornado IDS stores options

Above: Tornado IDS can carry most items of tactical air-to-surface ordnance in the NATO inventory, which ranges from small practice bombs to guided missiles and tactical nuclear weapons. There seems to be few limits on what the Panavia aircraft can carry – BAe has even studied the possible carriage of Stingray lightweight torpedoes.

1 Raketen-Technik MW-1 multipurpose submunitions dispenser
2 Hunting Engineering JP233 airfield attack dispenser
3 Matra/MBB Apache/CWS stand-off dispenser
4 MBB reconnaissance pod
5 Marconi Defence Systems ARI 23246/1 Sky Shadow ECM pod
6 Selenia ALQ-234 ECM pod
7 MBB Kormoran anti-ship missile
8 Bodenseewerk Gerätetechnik AIM-9L Sidewinder air-to-air missile
9 330 Imp gal (1,500 lit) fuel tank
10 Ford AIM-9B Sidewinder air-to-air missile
11 Hughes Aircraft AGM-65 Maverick air-to-surface missile
12 Aérospatiale AS.30 air-to-surface missile
13 BAe Sea Eagle anti-ship missile
14 Low-drag cluster bomb
15 BAe Alarm anti-radar missile
16 AVQ-23A Pave Spike TV tracker and laser designator/ranger
17 Mauser 27mm cannon and ammunition
18 ML Aviation CBLS 200 practice bomb carrier
19 Matra 400kg (880lb) laser-guided bomb
20 28lb (12.7kg) practice bomb
21 20lb (9kg) practice bomb
22 4lb (1.8kg) practice bomb
23 5lb (2.27kg) practice bomb
24 Texas Instruments Paveway II Mk 13/18 1,000lb (450kg) laser-guided bomb
25 1,000lb (450kg) general-purpose bomb
26 Napalm dispenser
27 Stores carrier
28 Tactical nuclear weapons
29 Rockwell International GBU-15 guided glide bomb
30 Matra/Thomson Brandt BLG 66 Belouga cluster bomb
31 Hunting Engineering BL 755 cluster bomb
32 Lepus flare
33 LR25 rocket pod

Deployment

For most operators of Tornado, the arrival of the Panavia warplane introduced two-seat cockpits with new levels of system complexity, transforming their front-line strength and increasing their striking power. When fully deployed Tornado will be the most powerful tactical strike force in the NATO inventory, while in the Gulf Tornados serving with the Royal Saudi and Sultan of Oman's Air Forces will be a warning to anyone casting envious eyes on the area's oil wealth. For the pilots of Israel's air force the type will be a potential opponent offering a disturbing challenge to that service's traditional combat skills.

From the earliest days of the Tornado programme, it had been hoped that the aircrew of all three nations would be trained at a single location. A Joint Operational Training Study Group tasked with investigating the feasibility of this studied the problem for three years before recommending in 1975 that a tri-national Tornado training establishment (TTTE) be set up.

An Aircrew Course Design team, established in the UK in May 1977, was initially staffed with RAF officers, and the first German personnel – a pilot and a navigator – joined in the following August. In May 1979 the team moved to RAF Cottesmore in England, the location chosen for the TTTE. Several months later it was augmented by two more German officers plus one from Italy.

Planning the training scheme raised novel problems. Each user had its own way of working, while its aircraft displayed minor but significant differences in equipment standard. Flight manuals and checklists would therefore have to incorporate cross-references and supplements to deal with these national differences.

Initial training of service instructors – nine pilots and six instructors – was handled by MBB under a Panavia contract. This took place at the Ottobrunn Development Centre and the Manching Flight Test Centre, starting in May 1980. By July, these first crews were airborne, and apparently enjoying every minute of the experience. "It's fun to fly, particularly this fly-by-wire system", said one trainee – Wing Commander Robert O'Brien, the man tasked with being Chief Flying Instructor of the TTTE. With less than half a dozen hours on the type, he was already enthusiastic. "It's going to be easy to convert to. There's no magic

surrounding it, and you don't need to be an astronaut. The young lads in the street who are going to become pilots will just fly it".

In the meantime the aircraft which the unit would need were taking shape. BT.001, the first production UK trainer, was assigned to Boscombe Down in November 1979, joining pre-series aircraft 12 and 15, while GT.001, the first production German trainer, arrived at Manching in the spring of 1980. On March 14, 1980, BAe Warton flew BS.001, the first production strike Tornado. This was followed by BS.002 (ZA322), the first strike aircraft delivered to the TTTE. In the summer of that year, after a spell at Boscombe Down, BT.002 (ZA320) – the first production trainer – also went to the TTTE. These were soon joined by German production aircraft, with GT.005 arriving on September 2 and GT.004 a day later. The first Italian-built aircraft was not to arrive at Cottesmore to join the TTTE until April 1982.

Having received its first production aircraft in July 1980, the unit's first job was to train further instructors, the MBB-trained crews trying out their training skills on personnel assigned to the unit as instructors. By January 1981 the new instructors had been instructed, and all was ready: the TTTE was officially opened, and the training of operational aircrew began.

The TTTE is organized in three flying squadrons commanded by British, German and Italian officers respectively. The post of Chief Flying Instructor alternates between an RAF Wing Commander and a German Lieutenant Colonel, while other leading posts are filled by officers from all three nations on a rotational basis. Costs are shared between the three European partners.

Below: Training at the TTTE is fully integrated, with crews of mixed nationality until final pairings are made and all instruction in English: the pilot preparing for a sortie in this German Tornado could be from any of the three nations involved.

Above: German, British and Italian Tornados G-73, B-55 and I-40 from the Trinational Tornado Training Establishment at RAF Cottesmore in formation soon after the arrival of the first Italian production aircraft in April 1982.

Trinational Tornado Training Establishment Aircraft

B-50 (British)

G-24 (German)

I-92 (Italian)

Aircraft at the TTTE are differentiated by national insignia and prefixes to the tail codes; numbers below 49 indicate aircraft with dual flight controls while 50 and above are applied to full IDS-standard machines.

Above: The flight line at Cottesmore in October 1981. At full strength, average complement is 50 aircraft, including 22 from Germany, 21 from the RAF and seven from Italy; the first Saudi aircrew arrived for training by the RAF in 1985.

Since the base is located in the UK, a substantial part of the UK contribution is provided in services rather than cash – most of the 1,900 personnel at Cottesmore are provided by the RAF.

The unit normally has around 50 aircraft, having reached full strength in August 1982. A typical mix would be 22 from Germany, 21 from the UK and seven from Italy. All carry the unit marking – a black arrowhead with a red outline, and bearing the initials TTTE – plus an alphanumeric designation consisting of the letter B, G or I (indicating nationality) plus a number. Strike aircraft have numbers running from 50 upwards; lower numbers indicate dual-control trainers.

Around 150 Tornado IDS aircrews are trained at the TTTE each year. ADV training is handled by another RAF unit, a sensible arrangement since the ADV is not in German or Italian service. The unit provides a fully integrated common training programme for conversion and familiarization with the Tornado, formation flying, navigation, terrain following and tactical training. All instruction is given in English, and it is common practice for students from one nation to be trained by instructors from another.

A typical trainee population would be around 20 German pilots and 10 navigators, a slightly smaller number from the UK, and perhaps six Italian pilots plus three navigators. Most of the early RAF crews to be assigned to the TTTE for training were ex-Buccaneer, while others had flown the Jaguar or Phantom, and were therefore used to two-seat operations. Luftwaffe personnel were mostly from F-104G units, so many lacked two-seat experience, while Italian crews had only single-cockpit F-104G, F-104S and G.91 experience.

The pattern of training used for the earliest classes was as follows: pilots flew nine sorties with a pilot instructor – around 9-13 hours in all – while navigator trainees flew 13 sorties. For pilots, this was followed by a similar period with a navigator instructor in the back seat. The final period of around nine sorties saw trainee pilot and navigator teamed up to create an all-new crew. At the end of the course, the new pilot would have flown around 35-40 hours on Tornado, while his back-seater would have clocked up 25-30 hours. This pattern has stood the test of time, and the crews leaving the TTTE at the end of their 13-week conversion course will have flown roughly the number of hours indicated above.

Being the first Tornado unit, the TTTE was naturally the centre of much interest as ground crews and aircrew came to grips with their new mount. Tornado introduced both to a new level of complexity, and the learning curve was a shallow one. Three years after the unit opened for business, aircraft serviceability was still only around 50 per cent, but this was partly due to shortage of spares – operational units enjoyed priority.

One facility at Cottesmore which attracted favourable comment was the RB199 Test House. Built into a former hangar by Marconi Avionics and Industrial Acoustics, it allows engines to be run on a testbed which incorporates an efficient noise-attenuation system. Engine instrumentation points are connected to the Marconi Automated Powerplant Test (APT) system. This monitors the data in real time, giving alarms in the event of any problems, displays the data (once again in real time) on colour video monitors, and prints hard-copy permanent records.

The computerized system cues the operator through the test procedure, and can even run a mathematical simulation of the engine which may be used for training purposes.

The Test House was a great success. Experience showed that engines could be moved into the facility and connected up to the APT electronics in only 30 minutes. With the RB199 running at full power, the noise level 650ft (200m) from the Test House was only 65dB. The RAF duly ordered similar systems for all its Tornado bases. The Italian Air Force was equally impressed, and promptly placed a similar order.

While the new crews were training at the TTTE back in 1981, their governments were re-thinking the shape of the Tornado programme. A fourth batch of 162 aircraft had been ordered in January of that year, but the aircraft was not in full production and the delivery rate was building at a time when national defence budgets were showing signs of strain. In 1981 the three lines were scheduled to deliver around 126 aircraft, and the pace was due to quicken. Under the original schedule, for example, UK production alone would have reached a rate of 63 aircraft per year in 1983.

Germany requested a slow-down in the production rate in order to trim its growing defence budget. Faced with its own financial problems, the UK was happy to agree, so the production pace was cut back and the programme stretched out in timescale. As a result, the 1981 output was less than 100 aircraft. Although promoted as a cost-saving exercise, this stretch-out would inevitably increase the final bill. According to BAe, the total cost of the programme would rise by £150 million, effectively increasing the cost of each aircraft delivered by 3.5 per cent.

Once trained crews became available, Tornado could take its place in the front line of the four user air arms. This process began in 1982 with deliveries to all four users – 13 years after project go-ahead. From this point the story of Tornado develops more on national lines, and can most easily be traced by describing its deployment by each nation in turn, starting with the first service to deploy the type operationally, Britain's Royal Air Force.

RAF weapons conversion

After completing TTTE training, RAF Tornado IDS crews are posted to the Tornado Weapons Conversion Unit (TWCU) at RAF Honington. Here they are introduced to the weapons and operational tactics they will use at their operational squadron. Pilots fly for around 32 hours, while the navigator flies for just under 30 hours. In addition to training new crews, the TWCU also runs a Weapons Instructor course.

The TWCU was formally opened on January 8, 1982, and played a major role in preparing the aircraft for front-line service. Run by Wing Commander Duncan Griffiths, and equipped with 22 aircraft, this unit soon showed what the Tornado could do. Average accuracy in loft bombing attacks was around 200ft (60m), while blind bombing attacks showed average figures of under 100ft (30m). Visual attacks were more dependent on pilot skill, but results showed that a good crew could plant its weapons within 75ft (23m) of the target.

TWCU personnel were delighted with the performance of the aircraft's radar. During radar-attack trials, crews dis-

Left: One of the three Tornados from the RAF TWCU that carried out the type's first overseas deployment by the service at Andrews AFB, Washington, DC, in May 1983.

covered that the radar imagery in the cockpit was clearly showing the position of a buried telephone cable close to the target – the radar was managing to obtain a usable signal from the 2in (5cm) high ridge of earth created when the cable was buried.

By March 1984 the TWCU had handled 17 courses, dropped more than 14,000 practice bombs and clocked up 10,000 accident-free flying hours. It had also carried out the first overseas deployment, sending three aircraft to the USA to participate alongside the Red Arrows aerobatic team at an air display at Andrews AFB in Washington DC.

Apart from its training role, the TWCU would be used as a combat unit in an international emergency, assuming the "shadow" designation No. 45 Sqn. All the unit's aircraft carry the TWCU insignia – a crown and sword superimposed on crossed arrows – on their vertical fin, but many also have No. 45 Sqn insignia on the forward fuselage. This takes the form of a winged camel flanked by red diamonds on a blue background and displaces the RAF roundels from their normal location to a position on the air inlet trunking.

UK-based strike aircraft form part of No. 1 Group. Having lost its six squadrons of Vulcan heavy bombers in the early 1980s, it is now equipping with several Tornado GR.1 squadrons. Squadron deliveries to the RAF started on January 6, 1982 with the handover of ZA586 to IX Sqn, a former Vulcan unit. This was based at Honington, alongside the TWCU. Six months later, on June 1, 1982, this unit became Strike Command's first operational Tornado squadron.

The next two RAF Tornado units to form were No. 617 Sqn, the Dam Busters, and No. 27 Sqn. Both operate from RAF Marham in Norfolk. No. 617 Sqn was officially formed on May 16, 1983, 40 years to the day after the Lancaster raid on the Ruhr dams which give the then newly-formed unit its name. No. 27 Sqn had its debut three months later, officially forming on August 12.

All three squadrons were soon dispatching their aircraft on overseas assignments. A single Tornado from No.

Above: Tornado of No. 9 Squadron, the RAF's first operational unit, based at RAF Honington, in flight with four 1,000lb (450kg) bombs and fuel tanks.

9 Sqn flew from the UK to Cyprus and back with support from a Victor K.2 tanker and the "buddy" refuelling pack on a Buccaneer S.2, carrying out a 520nm (965km) low-level flight en route.

No. 27 Sqn deployed to Thumrait in Oman for a ten-day visit in early 1984, stopping off at Dhahran in Saudi Arabia, and Abu Dhabi. While operating from RAF Laarbruch in West Germany, one of No. 27's crews was to accidentally demonstrate the need for a revised ejection procedure. On November 27, 1984, the aircraft had an unexpected

encounter near Schweinfurt with a USAF A-10 Thunderbolt, and the pilot pulled up sharply to avoid collision with the US aircraft. The navigator interpreted this manoeuvre as an indication that the fly-by-wire system had failed, so initiated command ejection.

As described in the Structure chapter, Command Ejection mode allows one crew member to eject the other. This ability of the pilot to eject his back-seater is a sensible precaution in an aircraft designed to fly at high speed close to the ground. Under normal circumstances, an ejection by the navigator will not affect the front seater unless a lever in the rear cockpit has been pushed to the forward position to select command ejection mode. On November 27, 1984, it was, and the pilot's reward for skilfully avoiding the A-10 was to find himself departing from his aircraft under the power of the Mk 10 ejection seat. The rules for command ejection were promptly altered: now, only in "exceptional circumstances" is the back-seater allowed to select command ejection mode.

First German-based RAF Tornado unit was No. 15 Sqn, which formed at Laarbruch in October 1984. It was soon joined by No. 16 Sqn, which formed at Laarbruch on February 29 of the following year. Although lacking the range of the Vulcan medium bomber, Tornado is positioned closer to its potential targets. It can thus act as an effective nuclear-delivery system. With their 750nm (1,390km) hi-lo-lo-hi tactical radius, German-based Tornados could hit targets in East Germany, Poland, and Hungary, and even penetrate around 110nm (200km) into Soviet airspace. Given support from Tornados equipped with "buddy" refuelling packs, it could strike deeper into the Western USSR. A reminder of this role came in 1984, when

RAF Germany modified its aircraft to carry tactical nuclear weapons.

Arrival of the Panavia fighter allowed the subsonic Buccaneer to be phased out of RAF service in Germany. Operated as an interim strike aircraft following the demise of the TSR.2 and AFVG programmes, this had proved a valuable addition to RAF strength. Some will be retained into the 1990s in the maritime strike role, serving with two Lossie-mouth-based squadrons which had originally been due to convert to Tornado.

Nos 15 and 16 Sqns were the first of the planned eight Tornado units of RAF Germany – seven GR.1 squadrons plus a reconnaissance unit. The two UK-based GR.1 squadrons will eventually be joined by a reconnaissance unit. Next to begin

Above left: Tornado ZA542 of No. 27 Squadron, based at RAF Marham and officially reformed in August 1983, was photographed in its squadron markings the previous April.

Left: No. 15 Squadron was the first Tornado unit to become operational with RAF Germany, being reformed in October 1984 at Laarbruch, where it had previously operated Buccaneers.

conversion was No. 20 Sqn. After moving from Bruggen, this Jaguar squadron disbanded in June 1984, but had already received the first of the Tornados with which it would re-form. As Jaguars are progressively withdrawn from RAF Germany, Nos 14, 17, and 31 Sqns will switch to Tornado, and be joined by No. 9 from the UK. No. 2 Sqn at Laarbruch will eventually reequip as a Tornado reconnaissance unit, while a second will be formed in the UK. By the time Tornado deployment ends, the aircraft will make up around two thirds of the RAF's front-line strength.

The RAF's IDS flight simulator was jointly developed by Rediffusion Simulation and the Link-Miles division of Singer (UK). The first was installed at Cottesmore in 1981, and was soon followed by the second. The remaining four were installed at operational bases – Honington, Cottesmore and Marham in the UK and Laarbruch in West Germany. Although the equipment incorporates a cockpit section complete with a three degrees of motion system, it is designed to be transportable. All its sections are housed in shelters, so a system can be broken down, moved to a new location, then re-assembled in only six weeks. This resulted in some economies, as one of the Cottesmore systems was earmarked for eventual use at Bruggen.

Luftwaffe and Marineflieger
First deliveries to West Germany started in February 1982, when aircraft began to arrive at the Erding-based weapons training unit (WaKo). In the summer of the following year the unit moved to Jever in northern Germany to form the nucleus of JaboG 38. The summer of 1983 saw JaboG 31 "Boelcke" – an F-104G unit based at Norvenich – converting to Tornado, with JaboG 32 at Lechfield (another F-104G unit) following in 1984. Also slated to convert in the future are the Starfighter-equipped JaboG 33 and

Below: Barbed wire and CBW-garbed personnel emphasise the serious purpose of RAF Germany Tornado bases such as Laarbruch, home of this No. 20 Squadron Tornado.

Right: A Tornado of No. 31 Squadron, one of four former Jaguar squadrons to fly the Tornado in RAF Germany, taxis out to the runway at Brüggen.

Below right: A Tornado of another of the Brüggen-based former Jaguar squadrons, No. 17, which, like all RAF Germany Tornado squadrons, is assigned to 2nd Allied Tactical Air Force under NATO command.

34. A training squadron will also equip with the type.

First Marineflieger unit to receive Tornado was MFG 1. Based at Leck and flying the F-104G, it began converting to the Tornado in July 1982. MFG 2 will also trade in its Starfighters for the Panavia warplane. Tasks of both units include strike missions against naval and coastal targets, plus reconnaissance.

Germany expects to complete the Tornado programme in 1987, by which time the Luftwaffe will have taken delivery of 212 aircraft, and 112 will have reached the Marineflieger. The Luftwaffe will then concentrate procurement efforts on the Roland and Patriot missiles in order to improve its SAM defences.

One problem faced by the West German Defence Ministry is a shortage of ordnance. According to a 15-year plan for defence spending submitted to the Bundestag, Tornado will be short of ordnance until the end of the century, by which point it will be half-way through its service life. In order to make funds available for weaponry both for Tornado and for Alpha Jet strike units, Germany has decided to postpone deployment of the first of 200 European Fighter Aircraft (EFA) from 1995 to 1997.

Aeronautica Militare Italiano
In Italian service, Tornado replaces the F-104G, although the improved F-104S will continue in the interceptor role until the mid-1990s. First Italian unit to receive Tornado was the 154° Gruppo (squadron) of the 6° Stormo (wing) at Brescia-Ghedi, the first examples arriving in the autumn of 1982. Next to convert was 156° Gruppo of 36° Stormo at Bari. By the time Italy has taken all 100 of its aircraft (99

plus the refurbished pre-series aircraft X-588), Tornado will equip a total of four Gruppos, including 155° at Ghedi and the 3° Gruppo Efficienza Velivoli, a maintenance unit based at Cameri, near Milan.

In August 1982, just as the first squadrons were entering operational service with all three nations, the fifth production batch was ordered. This consisted of 171 aircraft, including 52 ADVs. The sixth batch – originally intended to be the final consignment – was ordered almost 18 months later on January 7, 1984. This involved 155 aircraft, 63 IDS and 92 ADV, bringing the total production run to 805. Four of the pre-series aircraft would be updated to the full IDS production standard, raising the total to 809.

ADV deployment
By 1985 the RAF was forming its first Tornado ADV unit. Flight development of the ADV prior to first deliveries to the RAF involved 1,300 flight hours. BAe pilots were responsible for all but 250 hours of this work, the remainder being done by RAF crews. By the autumn of 1985 the rapid-rolling programme needed to clear the aircraft for service use had been completed, and Sidewinder firing trials, although still under way, were on schedule. Other trials were due to test zoom-climb performance at heights of up to 70,000ft (21,000m).

The Service Instructor Aircrew Training (SIAT) programme for the ADV took place at BAe Warton. Two courses were run, familiarizing the instructors of 299 OCU, the first unit to equip with the type, with the aircraft. These personnel then returned to RAF Coningsby – home base of 229 OCU – which took delivery of the first of a scheduled 16 aircraft in September 1984. These were built to the F.2 standard; production would be switched to the Mk 104-engined F.3 with the 19th aircraft. Full-mission and air-combat simulators for the ADV will be installed at Coningsby in 1987. The unit will also have a Cockpit Emergency and Procedure Trainer.

Initial service reaction to the aircraft has been favourable, with handling qualities and serviceability exceeding expectations, though the F.2 models had several deficiencies. Wing sweep had to be manually controlled, the second INS was not fitted, and computer capacity was still 64K. The most serious shortcoming involved the AI24 and the fact that few of these first aircraft had operational radars. The MoD had requested modifications to the first batch of radars, causing delays which resulted in most aircraft carrying either nose ballast or non-functioning radar sets. No details of the radar modifications have been released, though according to a report in *Flight International* the AI24 was being modified to increase signal-to-noise ratio, and a satisfactory fix has been devised.

These deficiencies did not hamper early training operations, since some of the unit's aircraft were dual-control models used for pilot conversion, and the

absence of radar on these was not important, while training sorties which required a functioning radar could be flown with the small number of radar-equipped aircraft.

The first front-line F.3 squadron is due to become operational in late 1986, and the RAF plans to deploy seven ADV squadrons, all part of No. 11 Group, with the last forming in 1991. In wartime, the OCU will act as an eighth squadron. Three squadrons will be based at RAF airfields in the UK – Coningsby, Leuchars and Leeming – but small numbers of aircraft are likely to be positoned at forward bases such as Stornoway on the Isle of Lewis.

Like earlier RAF aircraft, the ADVs will operate from hardened aircraft shelters. These will be a new third-generation design sized to accommodate two aircraft, and incorporating hardened annexes containing the fuel bowser and support equipment such as generators. The aircraft will be fuelled via pipework which runs beneath the floor of the shelter.

Normal CAP loading is two Sidewinder and two Sky Flash, plus two 490Imp gal (2,250lit) external tanks. Tornado F.2 flies during most of the time under direct autopilot control and with its wings at minimum sweep. Normal operating height while waiting for intruders would be 10,000-30,000ft (3,000-9,000m). The autopilot is able to fly the route to and from the selected CAP area, then fly the CAP holding pattern. Aircrew fatigue is thus minimized; an important consideration during long missions.

Once on station, the autopilot may be used to hold the aircraft in a CAP pattern in a fixed geographical location or positioned over a moving target such as a convoy of ships. The crew are thus free to concentrate their attention on searching for targets using the radar and ESM systems.

By the end of 1983 more than 300 aircraft had been delivered, and around 65,000 flight hours had been logged. The 400th aircraft was delivered in early 1985, and the 500th had been handed over by the start of 1986. Production was continuing at a rate of 110 aircraft per year – 44 from the BAe line, 42 from MBB and 24 from Aeritalia. At this rate production was due to end in 1989, long before the proposed EFA would be ready to take its place in the factories.

Behind the scenes, however, officials were already discussing a possible seventh production batch. At the 1984

Farnborough Air Show, BAe was talking in terms of around 100 extra aircraft being built, some for export and others as attrition replacement, though many of the journalists attending the show must have regarded BAe assurances that export deals were about to come to fruition with a degree of polite scepticism: up to that time Tornado's track record in the export stakes had been a disaster.

Export competition

By the mid-1980s Australia and Canada were both shopping for new fighters. Australia needed to replace its fleet of

Above: Luftwaffe Tornado 44+17 in the markings of Jagdbombergeschwader (JaBoG) 38 and wearing the new colour scheme of dark grey, dark green and medium green.

Mirage IIIO fighters, and had an initial requirement for 42 aircraft, while Canada needed between 120 and 150 to replace its CF-5, CF-101 Voodoo and CF-104 Starfighter fleets. Both were looking for long-range fighters able to operate out of a limited number of airfields. The competition was severe, and included the F-14, F-15, F-16, F/A-18, F-18L and Mirage F1.

By November 1978 Tornado had been dropped from the shortlists of both nations, with high unit cost apparently having acted against the Panavia aircraft. Hard figures are difficult to obtain, and depend (like all published aircraft costs) on the accounting basis being used, but a realistic system cost for the IDS is probably around $25 million, with the F.2 proving more expensive at around $27 million. Australia and Canada were both to opt for the McDonnell-Douglas F/A-18 Hornet.

By this time Tornado was in the running for an even more lucrative order – the USAF was looking for a new tactical fighter able to operate in all weathers, supplementing the F-111. Tornado was the only off-the-shelf candidate, becoming a contender in the Enhanced Tactical Fighter programme in October 1978, and in March of the following year, Panavia teamed with Grumman to offer the aircraft to the USAF. USAF pilots flew the aircraft, and seemed impressed by its capabilities, but the ETF requirement was eventually shelved, and the USAF was eventually to order the F-15E dual-role version of the Eagle.

Spain was the next nation to consider Tornado, but once again the order went to McDonnell-Douglas and the F/A-18, and when Greece showed serious interest Panavia pulled out all the stops in an attempt to clinch the order, forseeing the possible sale of up to 60 aircraft. The Greek Air Force was obviously attracted by the aircraft's capability, while the local aerospace industry was an obvious target for a co-production deal, and at the 1982 Defendory defence exibition at Piraeus, in Greece, Panavia was one of the few companies to have prepared the graphics and displays on its stand in Greek rather than English. Greece was offered

a substantial offset deal which would have included co-production, making Hellenic Aerospace Industries a fourth partner in the programme.

By the autumn of 1984, however, history seemed to be repeating itself as Greece announced that Tornado had been dropped from the shortlist, which now consisted of the F-16C, F/A-18A and Mirage 2000. High unit cost, and the better air-to-air combat potential of the alternatives, were unofficially cited as reasons for rejecting the European fighter. After repeatedly postponing a decision, Greece finally opted later in 1984 to order the F-16 and Mirage.

Left: Luftwaffe Tornado 44+43 of JaBoG 32, which reformed at Lechfeld, southern Germany, in August 1984, and, along with JaBoG 33 at Buchel, is assigned to 4th Allied Tactical Air Force; JaBoG 31, based at Nörvenich, is, like the RAF Germany Tornado squadrons, assigned to NATO's 2ATAF.

Below: Port side view of the same aircraft; pylon and tank have not been repainted in the new colours.

Middle Eastern interest

By 1984, Panavia was focussing most of its marketing efforts on two Middle East nations, Oman and Saudi Arabia. At Farnborough that year BAe was confidently predicting export sales of up to 100 aircraft, 60 or more to Saudi Arabia, and between 30 and 40 to Oman.

Back in 1982 Saudi Arabia had expressed interest in a batch of at least 40 Tornado IDS – enough for two squadrons – to supplement the 60 F-15 interceptors then being delivered as replacements for obsolescent BAC Lightnings. In theory, the best solution to the Royal Saudi Air Force's strike requirement would have been the purchase of additional F-15s fitted with conformal fuel tanks and multiple bomb ejection racks, and the Saudi government had asked for such tanks and bomb racks to be included in the original deal, but the strong pro-Israeli faction in the US Congress was able to ensure that this equipment was not supplied. The US government also insisted that the Eagles should not be deployed to Tabuk air base, which is in the northwestern part of the country and close to Israel.

In 1984 the Saudi Government once again approached the US government, indicating a desire to purchase between 25 and 40 new F-15s, either the single-seat F-15C or the planned dual-role F-15E two-seater, and to co-produce between 80 and 120 F-20A Tigersharks as replacements for the F-5E force. The supply of conformal fuel tanks and MER-200 multiple ejection bomb racks was again requested, but despite Saudi insistence that it would shop elsewhere if refused the equipment it wanted, the pro-Israeli lobby predictably opposed the planned deal.

Behind the scenes, the Saudis had already started negotiating with Britain for Tornado fighters and Hawk trainers, and with France for a possible Mirage 2000 purchase. Evidence that their intentions were serious emerged when a Royal Saudi Air Force evaluation team flew several Tornado IDS sorties from RAF Honington in 1984.

By mid-1984 rumours around the defence industry reported that a Tornado sale was imminent, and even that a letter of intent had been signed in June, but by the end of the year "Tornado fever" had died away, and it seemed that the shorter-ranged Mirage 2000 might be chosen. France was reported to be negotiating a deal in which between 40 and 50 Mirage 2000 fighters would be bartered for Saudi oil. Some rumours ascribed the supposed Saudi rejection of Tornado to the aircraft's high price, while others hinted at a deterioration of relations, for various reasons, between Saudi Arabia and the UK.

Negotiations with the other likely customer, the Sultanate of Oman, involved fewer political problems. Oman's

Above: First Marineflieger Tornado squadron, reformed at Schleswig-Jagel in July 1982, was MFG1, one of whose aircraft is seen here deploying its buddy refuelling system.

strategic location on the Strait of Hormuz, the narrow waterway through which almost half the oil needed by the industrial world must pass, makes it a natural target for avaricious eyes: an Oman government hostile to the West could base heavy artillery on Omani islands in the Strait, making them impassable to oil tankers.

In the early 1980s the greatest threat faced by Sultan Qaboos was posed by Iran, whose ruler, Ayatollah Khomeini, would like to see Islamic fundamentalist governments taking power in the six pro-Western states in the area – Bahrain, Kuwait, Oman, Qatar, Saudi Arabia and the United Arab Emirates. In 1984 these nations formed the Gulf Co-operation Council (GCC) to coordinate their military planning. Oman also has financial and security agreements with Islamic countries such as Jordan and Pakistan, which have internationally recognized military expertise. One of the first GCC projects, in April 1984, was to provide Bahrain and Oman, whose oil revenues are much smaller than those of the other four allies, with a billion dollars in aid to be spent on military equipment and training.

For many years, the main combat aircraft in Omani service was the subsonic Hawker Siddeley Hunter FGA.9. Of the 31 originally supplied, 18 remain in service at Thumrayt air base, while others are in storage. Most of the operational Hunters are ex-Jordanian Air Force FGA.76 single-seat fighters, updated with AIM-9P Sidewinder; some are equipped for photo reconnaissance, while for training four two-seaters are available – two ex-Jordanian Air Force T.66B and two ex-Kuwaiti Air Force T.67.

In 1974 Oman ordered 12 Jaguar strike aircraft from the UK at a total cost of around $83 million. Delivery was completed in 1978, the aircraft being deployed as a single squadron based at Thumrayt. A second batch of 12, ordered in 1980, was delivered by the end of 1983, along with a two-seat trainer built on the Indian production line, and used to create a new squadron based at Masirah air base.

Faced with the political tensions in the region, Sultan Qaboos decided in the late 1970s to upgrade his armed forces. Oman has strong military links with the

West, including the USA, Britain and France. Between 1978 and 1982, Oman spent $460 million in the UK, $60 million in the USA, $10 million in France, and around $20 million with other arms suppliers – a total of $550 million. In addition to the Jaguars, new equipment taken into service included fast patrol boats from Britain plus French-built Exocet missiles to arm them, and military helicopters and transports from the USA. Defence now accounts for about 40 per cent of the national budget.

In the 1960s and 1970s Oman had not received US military assistance or credits, but in June 1980 President Carter decided to provide around $50 million in military credits over the next two fiscal years. This process has continued under President Reagan, with $60 million being granted in FY82 and FY83 and more over the next three years.

Sultan Qaboos has taken the step (seen by some as a calculated political risk) of providing base and refuelling facilities for the US Central Command (CENCOM), formerly known as the Rapid Deployment Force. If the latter were to be deployed to the area, the five major air bases of the Sultan of Oman's Air Force (SOAF) would be able to provide air cover for the US forces. The Sultan also agreed to allow the US government to stockpile military equipment at two of its airfields for use by the RDF in the event of a military emergency in the region.

Jaguar International is a flexible multi-role aircraft, but the basic design was conceived for the strike mission, and by the standards of the F-14, F-15, F-16, MiG-21 and MiG-23 fighters being flown by other air arms in the region, it is hardly the ideal interceptor, having a top speed of only Mach 1.6. Accordingly, the SOAF decided to purchase a suitable interceptor. As the Jaguar deals had shown, the number of aircraft involved would be small, but the evaluation was made with care. Types examined included the F-15, F-16 and Tornado ADV, and since the ADV was a UK project, negotiations with Oman were conducted by BAe.

Below: Kormoran-armed Tornado of the Aeronautica Militare Italiano's 156° Gruppo of the 36° Stormo, based at Gioia del Colle, where one flight is dedicated to the anti-shipping role, the base being close to the ports of Bari and Taranto.

Above: A pair of Italian Tornados from the 154° Gruppo of the 6° Stormo, based at Ghedi, near Brescia, display clean undersides during a photographic sortie over the Alps.

As time dragged on, and rumour followed rumour, the prospect of a Tornado sale to either nation seemed dim – the first draft of this chapter concluded with the words, "Although both the IDS and ADV are still being offered for export, they have attracted no orders to date".

In August 1985, however, the first export order was finally announced, when Oman signed for Tornado ADV, though instead of the 16 aircraft being predicted by many sources, the order was for only eight ADVs. Despite the

modest number of aircraft involved, the deal was worth more than £250 million, and included supply of training, support and Sky Flash missiles. Although covered by the UK Export Credits and Guarantee Department, the Tornado deal is probably being funded partly by the Gulf Co-operation Council, with Saudi Arabia perhaps providing further financial assistance.

The eight aircraft will be delivered by 1987. The Omani Air Force wants the fighters to be built to full RAF F.3 standards, and the eight will in fact be diverted from the RAF order. This small fleet is hardly large enough to form a viable squadron, so it is hardly surprising that an option for additional aircraft was included in the order.

An expanding air force needs better ground facilities, but work had already started on these as part of Oman's military build-up of the late 1970s and early 1980s. The SOAF has expanded and modernized its main operating bases – Masirah, Seeb, Khasab and Thumrayt – and operational, maintenance, storage and initial personnel-support facilities are all being improved. At Seeb and Thumrayt, for example, six hardened aircraft shelters, dispersal and access pavements, an environmentally controlled warehouse, and support areas are being built, plus storage facilities and transient billets for use in an emergency by US CENCOM units. New Omani Navy facilities were also built; some (such as an aircraft maintenance unit, a ground-support equipment shop, a warehouse facility and an ammunition magazine) are jointly used by the Navy and Air Force. Much of this construction work has been US-financed. Since 1980, the USA has provided more than $253 million in modernization funds, and is expected to give further assistance totalling $198 million by the late 1980s.

Saudi Arabian order

Selection of the Tornado by Oman was widely regarded as strengthening the aircraft's position in Saudi Arabia, with the impending sale of 48 IDS plus Hawk trainers being rumoured. A month after the Omani order, Saudi Defence Minister Prince Sultan bin Abdul-Aziz al Saud signed the biggest arms deal ever won by the UK – a £4,000 million package which included not only 48 IDS and 30 Hawks, but also 23 Tornado ADVs and 30 Swiss-built Pilatus PC-9 turboprop-powered trainers. This deal would be partly paid in cash, and partly in oil and was expected to lead to various collaborative industrial ventures by the two nations.

Reaction from Israel to the Omani and Saudi orders was predictably furious, but was unable to affect either sale. Mrs Thatcher's Conservative government

AMI Tornado 6-02 in the markings of the 154° Gruppo of the 6° Stormo. This unit served initially as the Italian Air Force's weapons training unit; ultimately, all three Italian Tornado Gruppi will be assigned to NATO's 5ATAF.

was probably in no mood to listen, given the speed with which Israel had rushed to re-arm Argentina after the 1982 Falklands War.

By the end of October 1985, the first Royal Saudi Air Force aircrew were training at RAF Cottesmore. Since the deal was struck with the UK, they were trained not by the tri-national TTTE, but by RAF instructors and on RAF aircraft. This was seen as a short-term solution; a training base will eventually be set up in Saudi Arabia. The UK Government placed no restrictions on how the aircraft should be deployed, raising the possibility that part of the force could eventually be stationed at Tabuk air base.

Deliveries of Tornado aircraft to the RSAF were to begin in March 1986, with 20 IDS aircraft originally ordered for the RAF being diverted to the new customer at the rate of around four per month. The aircraft would be delivered with full RAF-standard avionics, complete with weapons such as JP233 and Alarm once these became available. The ADVs would follow later, and be supplied with Sky Flash.

The Saudi deal was originally seen by Britain's Royal Air Force as injecting a useful delay into the British deployment pattern, allowing the service, already short of aircrew, to train the extra personnel it required for Tornado ADV and the final two IDS squadrons. (By 1984 the RAF was short of around 200 pilots, a figure which had risen to 250 by November 1985, when it was reported that 187

Below: Tornado F.2s of the RAF's No. 229 Operational Conversion Unit, which received its first aircraft in 1984 and which will be responsible for training aircrew for the 165 interceptor variants currently on order for Strike Commands No. 11 Group.

pilots had already left the service that year, around twice the number who had left in 1984. The cost to the UK taxpayer of these retirements was around £100 million. The already low manning level of 1.4 pilots per aircraft consequently fell to only 1.2, a figure which could worsen if more crews leave the service in 1986 and 1987, lured by the attractions of jobs in civil aviation or in Saudi Arabia.)

The RAF had realized that some aircrew would have to be seconded to the Gulf to support the Omani and Saudi deployments, but by late 1985 it was becoming obvious that the Saudi Air Force would probably rely on UK aircrew to man half its Tornados during the first five years of service, a figure of around 30 pilots plus 30 navigators being reported. Instead of the breathing space for which it had hoped, the RAF now found itself confronted by the loss of yet more aircrew, as flying personnel contemplated the prospects of lucrative three-year contracts with the RSAF.

Given these two contracts, Tornado's prospect of gaining further orders was bound to grow, particularly in the face of moves by the Gulf states to increase their level of defence collaboration. Jordan seemed the most likely prospect, with Tornado ADV joining the Mirage 2000 and F-20 Tigershark as a competitor for the RJAF's new interceptor requirement.

Within days of the US Senate voting by 92 to 1 to shelve a proposed arms deal with Jordan – 40 F-16 or F-20 fighters plus Sidewinder missiles and Improved Hawk and Stinger SAMs – it was reported that Jordan had asked the Saudi Government to add between 8 and 10 ADVs to its order for transfer to Jordan. The UK government seems to have refused this indirect deal, but clearly did not rule out a direct sale: by the end of the year, Jordanian aircrew were in the

UK test-flying both the IDS and ADV, and negotiations had begun with the Soviet Union on the possible supply of the MiG-29 'Fulcrum'.

Jordan lacks the oil wealth of its Arab neighbours, so often relies on friendly nations bankrolling its major arms deals. Its previous major aircraft order – 35 Mirage F1.C fighters – had been funded by Iraq, but the high cost of the war with Iran made Iraq an unlikely source of cash for further aircraft. Saudi Arabia seemed a more likely source of assistance.

Kuwait is seen as the other potential Tornado user in the Gulf area. A member of the Gulf Cooperation Council, it formerly operated the BAC Lightning, and currently fields a single Mirage F1 squadron and two squadrons of A-4KU Skyhawks.

Gulf cooperation

Collaboration by the Gulf Cooperation Council allies continues to develop. In November 1984 the participants agreed to a collective military alliance to combat against any external threat to any of the member states. Unlike NATO, this does not involve multi-national deployment of military units permanently stationed in the territory of one or more of the partners. Instead, the GCC has in mind an Arab rapid deployment force which could be fielded under a unified command. The GCC has also considered setting up a multi-national AEW force along the lines of the NATO E-3 Sentry fleet. The logical candidates were the E-3 – already in service in Saudi Arabia – or the Grumman E-2C Hawkeye.

The only other NATO nation seen as a likely Tornado user is Turkey, which was reported late in 1984 to be considering a 40-aircraft order. Turkey currently operates a collection of elderly types, many of which were acquired second-

hand; main front-line types are the F-104 Starfighter and the F-4 Phantom. The Turkish armed forces are desperately short of modern equipment, but even shorter of the funds needed for large-scale purchases of equipment. In 1987, the Turkish Air Force will take delivery of the first of 160 F110-powered F-16C fighters. The service also plans to buy more Sidewinders for its fighter force, and plans to procure a new generation air-to-air missile at a later date.

Faced with these programmes, the budget for new air force equipment is limited. Early in 1985 the UK Export Credits and Guarantee Department declined to finance a Turkish Tornado order, so the deal was stalled while BAe attempted to arrange alternative financing; discussions were still at an early stage in the autumn of 1985. Turkey is also reported to want Grumman E-2C Hawkeye AEW aircraft, but either deal would probably depend on an external source of funds or credit.

Another possible Tornado operator is Japan, which requires a replacement for the Mitsubishi F1 strike fighter. The F/A-18, F-16XL, AV-8B and Mirage 2000 are all reported to be under consideration, along with proposals for an indigenous FSX design powered by two Pratt & Whitney PW1120 engines. Panavia has put forward proposals for the direct purchase of 24 aircraft, plus options for a further buy of up to 76 examples. This deal would presumably involve local assembly, and some degree of local manufacture including offset work.

The only other nation known to have expressed a serious interest in Tornado in recent years is Iraq, which evaluated Tornado IDS in 1982 and discussed a possible order for up to 100, but the current war with Iran makes it unlikely that such an order would be accepted.

Operational Employment

Tornado is Western Europe's most important battlefield interdiction and deep strike aircraft; and the ADV version will be the United Kingdom's primary defence against air attack. Details of tactics and performance are, therefore, closely guarded, but by the end of 1985, with the IDS deployed in strength with four air arms in three countries, and the RAF's ADV Operational Conversion Unit building up to full strength, it was possible to gain some insights into methods of employment. Space precludes full consideration of the reconnaissance and anti-shipping roles, but the primary missions – strike and interception – are outlined, with the two major variants of necessity dealt with separately.

Tornado IDS

The roles envisaged for the Tornado IDS are counter-air, interdiction, anti-shipping, reconnaissance and, possibly, close air support. Of these, the first two are probably the most important and certainly the most difficult, at least in the context of a war in central Europe. The greatest threat to NATO forces is posed by Warsaw Pact air elements, which in recent years have developed into a force capable of mounting independent air operations over long distances and wide areas. They also have a considerable numerical advantage over the combined NATO air forces.

Despite the recent concentration on air superiority fighters by the Western nations, air power is best countered on the ground, where it is at its most vulnerable. Aircraft depend on fuel, weapons, maintenance, back-up services generally and, to a lesser degree, on hard runways. If some or all of these facilities can be damaged or destroyed much of their offensive capability is lost. The same reasoning applies to ground forces; they are dependent on supplies and reinforcements, without which the impetus of their attack cannot be sustained.

In the counter-air mission, therefore, the enemy airfield is the prime target, while interdiction targets would include choke points, typically bridges across rivers, and concentration areas for reinforcements. Optimized weapons have been designed to deal with all of these; the hard part is delivering them on target and returning safely to base, which means circumventing the enemy air defences. The Tornado IDS is almost certainly the world's most effective aircraft in this role, and permits its crews considerable flexibility in carrying out attacks.

The first stage lies in the mission planning. Once the target has been allocated the route out and back is planned to avoid known high risk areas. Friendly air defence zones are another potential hazard, and liaison with other friendly units is necessary to avoid the embarrassment of an outbound force meeting an incoming one at low level, especially at night or in bad weather. An element of deception will give unpredictability to the strike force, keeping the defenders guessing as to the target until the last possible moment and increasing the difficulty of interception, and terrain masking is also used where feasible.

Each squadron headquarters has a flight planning computer, complete with map board, cursor, keyboard and VDU. The navigator plots his intended route on the map, then feeds it into the computer along with waypoints, fixed radar-significant points (masts are particularly good), and other flight data. The computer then transfers the complete information for the flight plan on to a cassette, similar to the type used in tape recorders, and if necessary several identical flight plans can be turned out, each on its own cassette. The cassette is then installed in the Tornado cockpit.

In flight, Tornado's main computer will look at the distance to go to the next turning point and, using real time, will tell the crew when they will arrive at that point. The computer knows very accurately the ground speed, so if they plan to fly at a specific speed, say 420kt (778km/h), the crew can fly on a planned time line. Consequently they always have an indication of whether they are early or late against the planned ground speed. The early/late readings are extremely accurate. The crew also have a digital read-out of how far off track they are. The navigational kit gives an accuracy of less than one mile per hour error, with the INS and the Doppler constantly comparing their values.

When planning the route, the Tornado crew would consider using radar two or three times on the way to the range, or on the way to a real target, to update the navigational kit. They would use a radar-significant point, such as a mast, whose exact position would be pre-recorded on the cassette with the other data. When the aircraft was a few miles from that mast the crew would paint it on the radar, trying to avoid painting the ground and so getting a lot of unwanted returns. They would then slew the marker cross (on the display) over the top of the radar return, and insert the fix information into the navigation kit. The moment the button is pressed, the computer indicates the relative position of the mast from the aircraft, permitting accurate update of the kit.

All-weather formation flying

The navigation system also allows the aircraft to be flown in accurate formation, even when they are not in visual contact. They can fly in formation in cloud or darkness all the way, because the system gives the time early/late, as well as a very accurate track position on the digital read-out.

The basic concept of flying in formation to give each other mutual support has not changed since World War II. When Tornados fly in pairs, it could be in battle formation, and on a clear day the separation would vary according to the visibility, modified by the likely missile threat from opposing fighters. If the visibility was good, the spacing could be a couple of miles between aircraft, but in Northern Europe the average visibility is about five miles (8km) and often less, so the aircraft would not want to be too far apart because they could not then mutually support each other. Formation spacing is basically a function of two factors, visibility and aircraft threat – for example a Flogger's missile capability.

If Tornados are seen on the way out, their tremendous low-level speed might enable them to sneak past enemy fighters, though with a full load of weapons the Tornados would obviously not be so manoeuvrable. Flying very fast and very low, they would be a difficult target; and they could employ a variety of defensive measures. Night or bad weather would also provide some natural protection from WARPAC optically guided SAMs and aircraft systems.

On the way back Tornados could be much more aggressive, especially since they carry Sidewinders. One of the great points of Tornado is that the pilot can concentrate on flying fast and low while the navigator looks after the systems and fights the ECM battle. But so much is done by the computer, that even the navigator can spend far more of his time looking out.

Attacking Tornados have the ability to fly out and back in pre-planned and constant formations, and also have the capability of attacking the target without ever seeing it. Turning in formation needs much care, and a lot of time has been spent calculating the procedures for avoiding midair collisions. There is no

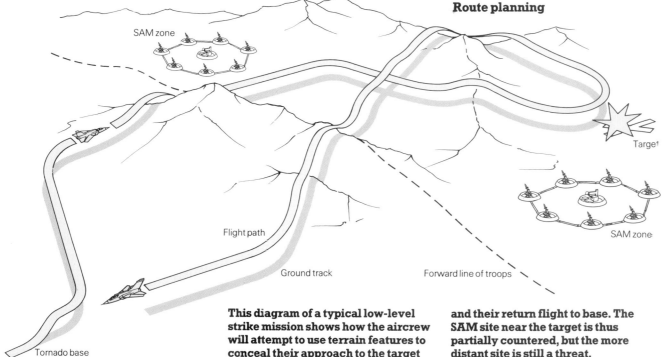

Route planning

This diagram of a typical low-level strike mission shows how the aircrew will attempt to use terrain features to conceal their approach to the target and their return flight to base. The SAM site near the target is thus partially countered, but the more distant site is still a threat.

SAM zone

Target

SAM zone

Flight path

Ground track

Forward line of troops

Tornado base

Left: The high velocity with which submunitions leave the MW-1 dispenser may be judged by their near-level trajectory in this head-on photo. The high initial impetus ensures they are widely scattered.

Right: Tornado GR.1 of 20 Sqn in a hardened shelter at RAF Laarbruch. Note the metal lining of the roof; this is designed to protect against spalling – fragmentation of the concrete outer shell – after bomb hits.

Below: Two Tornado GR.1s of 9 Sqn RAF release 1,000lb (450kg) retarded bombs. The tail-mounted drag chutes slow the bombs, allowing the aircraft to reach a safe distance before the weapons impact and detonate.

Bottom: Peacetime safety and noise regulations prevent these 9 Sqn aircraft from RAF Honington from flying at operational speeds and heights. Payload on this mission is four Mk 13/18 bombs plus ECM pods.

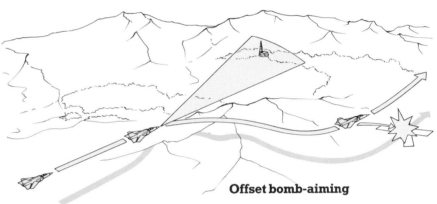

Offset bomb-aiming

If a target is unlikely to show up clearly on radar, the crew can opt to carry out an offset attack. When planning the sortie, they choose a radar-prominent object close to the target (in this case a pylon), loading its coordinates into the nav-attack system along with those of the target. A radar fix taken on the pylon can then be used for weapon aiming.

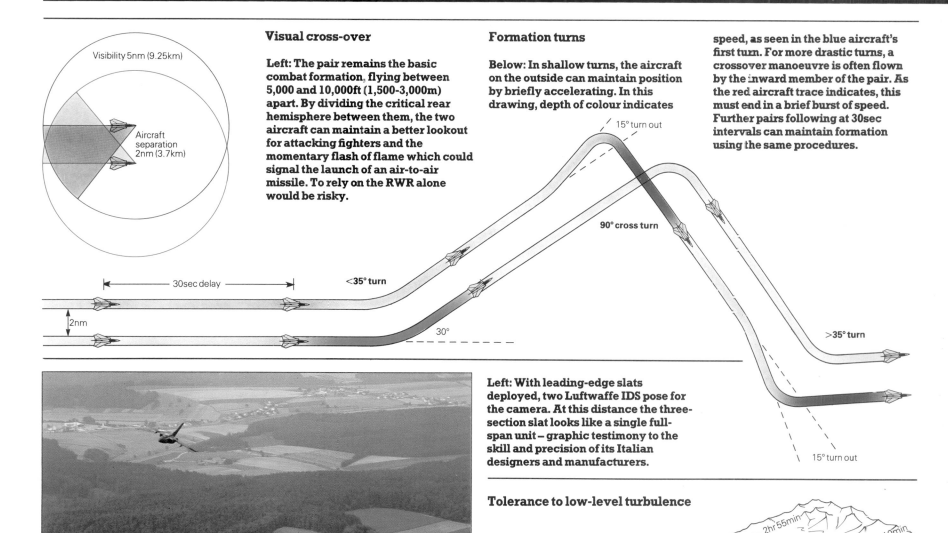

Visual cross-over

Left: The pair remains the basic combat formation, flying between 5,000 and 10,000ft (1,500-3,000m) apart. By dividing the critical rear hemisphere between them, the two aircraft can maintain a better lookout for attacking fighters and the momentary flash of flame which could signal the launch of an air-to-air missile. To rely on the RWR alone would be risky.

Formation turns

Below: In shallow turns, the aircraft on the outside can maintain position by briefly accelerating. In this drawing, depth of colour indicates speed, as seen in the blue aircraft's first turn. For more drastic turns, a crossover manoeuvre is often flown by the inward member of the pair. As the red aircraft trace indicates, this must end in a brief burst of speed. Further pairs following at 30sec intervals can maintain formation using the same procedures.

Visibility 5nm (9.25km)

Aircraft separation 2nm (3.7km)

30sec delay

2nm

<35° turn

90° cross turn

15° turn out

30°

>35° turn

15° turn out

Left: With leading-edge slats deployed, two Luftwaffe IDS pose for the camera. At this distance the three-section slat looks like a single full-span unit – graphic testimony to the skill and precision of its Italian designers and manufacturers.

Tolerance to low-level turbulence

2hr 55min
4hr 10min
1hr 07min
1hr 02min
Mach 0.7
2hr 05min
2hr 30min
Mach 0.9
500ft
F-4
F-104
Tornado
500ft (150m)
F-4
F-104
Tornado

According to Panavia, the maximum tolerable exposure time to low-altitude turbulence in Tornado is far longer than for the F-4 or F-104.

real problem in turning through angles of less than 35°, but more than that and the geometry of the turn would be such as to alter the formation. Depending on the speed and the spacing, the aircraft on the outside of the turn would have to accelerate. Conversely, aircraft on the inside may have to decelerate by a certain amount during the turn. For any turn it's basically a question of drawing it out geometrically, then calculating how to achieve sufficient separation between the individual aircraft.

Cross turns are also possible. If the outside aircraft of a pair turns outward,

away from the direction of the turn, by about 15° at 10 miles (18.5km) the inside aircraft can turn. Then the outside Tornado can roll out and reverse its turn, and still have in excess of ten seconds of separation. If the inside Tornado flies a constant time line while the outside aircraft, by turning away, generates an indication to show that it is always going to be 10 seconds late or whatever, then the inside Tornado is always going to be a mile and a half (2.75km) clear, which is all that is needed. So the outside aircraft doesn't even have to pull high; provided it turns away early, then rolls back and

turns through the inside, it will always end up back in formation having cleared the other aircraft by some 10 seconds, or whatever is wanted. This is also possible with multiple-aircraft formations.

Terrain-following flight

Another vital system is the terrain-following radar. It is optimized down to 200ft (60m) at Mach 0.9, which is really impressive, and it can be selected so that pilots can sit hands-off and get flown over mountains. Initially it can be mind-boggling to aircrew, but they soon become confident in its abilities.

In the rear cockpit is a digital read-out of the height above ground, and if you set 200ft (60m) then it never goes below 200ft. There are several self-protection schemes which result in an automatic pull-up. On a clear day TFR may not be used at all, but in bad weather or at night it is preferable to fly really low with it on and risk detection rather than stay at 1,000ft (300m) where the aircraft would be cannon fodder for all the SAM systems. There would be an awful lot of radar transmission going on so it could take some time for an enemy monitoring station to identify the TFR and start tracking it.

Tornado also has a ground mapping radar which is similar to that in the F-111, and that poses similar potential problems of announcing position to the enemy. The radar can be used in short bursts, however, to gain all the information aircrew need.

In a real war the number of radar transmissions from air and land is going to be phenomenal. If a Tornado were being illuminated by radar at low level, it might possibly be by a radar system that is dedicated to looking at it, in which case it could try to fly lower and see if it could use terrain masking. If the aircrew

Left: By fitting some Tornado IDS with 'buddy' refuelling packs, the RAF could penetrate deep into heavily defended airspace. Attrition among the large number of tankers needed to support a small number of strike aircraft would make very long range missions a rarity reserved for the highest-value targets.

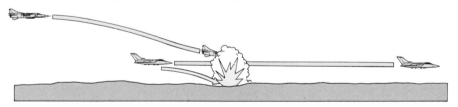

Emergency pusuit evasion

The use of retarded bombs allows Tornado to get well clear of blast and debris, but could spell trouble for a pursuing fighter. The deliberate release of a bomb at low level is an accepted last-ditch tactic which reduces payload but may persuade a pursuer to break off the chase.

had a warning that something was tracking them, then they could manoeuvre to break contact. Tornado's Skyshadow ECM pod has programs written to identify enemy radars and could send out signals to counter them. Tornado also carries chaff and flares to defeat missile systems in the BOZ-107 pod.

Tornado attack would be planned to utilize the aircraft's capability of dropping the weapons on time and very accurately, probably in formations so that a whole lot of aircraft arrive over the target at very short intervals, saturating the defences. With any SAM system it is basically easy to track a single aircraft, but with four, or eight, or even more, using a coordinated attack, the attacker's chances of survival are greatly increased.

Aircraft could all come in from different directions to confuse the ground defences, even from behind them, heading West, but this would carry a penalty in fuel, and also increase the time that the

aircraft were at risk to the ground defences.

Bombing competition success

"Very impressive": this is an expression that recurs over and over in descriptions of the Tornado GR.1. In 1984, crews from No. 617 Squadron took part in the United States Strategic Air Command Bombing and Navigation Competition, the first time Tornados had taken part. They took both first and second places in the Curtis E. LeMay Trophy for the highest scoring crews in high and low level bombing and time control; won the John C. Meyer Trophy for the highest damage expectancy; and came a very close second in the Mathis Trophy for most points in both high and low level bombing. Successful Tornado pilot Sqn Ldr Peter Dunlop summed up his mount in two words: "Absolutely marvellous".

The competition involved three sorties, each of roughly six hours' duration, one of which was by night, against simu-

Top: To the geologist it's a residual mountain, to the movie buff it's the setting for the climactic sequence in the film *Close Encounters of the Third Kind*, but to the crew of this 27 Sqn Tornado GR.1 it was probably just a convenient if spectacular navigational waypoint.

lated SAMs and interceptors, and using in-flight refuelling. Such is the accuracy of Tornado's navigation system that the average timing error on about 30 releases was less than one second, while the average mean point of impact of bombs dropped at very high speed and low level was less than 60ft (18m) from the target.

In the 1985 competition No. 27 Squadron Tornados did even better, repeating No. 617's success in the LeMay and Meyer trophies and scoring three second places for precision flying and bombing. The opposition comprised USAF B-52s, FB-111s and F-111s flown by

Above: The four Kormoran missiles carried by this Marineflieger Tornado could dispose of four enemy warships. As the number and effectiveness of minor naval vessels continues to increase, this sort of firepower is needed to ensure the success of over-water missions.

34 crews, and the Tornado aircrew came back convinced that in future competitions they would give even B-1Bs a good run for their money.

Tornado IDS has many more tricks up its sleeve, mainly to do with stand-off weapons and defence suppression munitions such as Harm and Alarm. Carrying anti-shipping missiles such as Sea Eagle or Kormoran it is also deadly against hostile naval units. This is the role for which it has been adopted by the *Marineflieger*, and its low-flying and time early/late kit will allow it to perform some really confusing (for the enemy) attack profiles.

Tornado ADV

The Tornado Air Defence Variant was designed specifically to defend the United Kingdom Air Defence Region. This vast area extends far beyond the coastline of the British Isles and covers nearly all the North Sea, a fair distance across the Denmark Strait towards Iceland, and the Western and Southwestern Approaches. Not so many years ago the threat sectors were considered to be the north and east, but the comparatively recent advent of fast, long-range Soviet aircraft armed with long-range cruise missiles has imposed a requirement for all-round defensive capability.

The threat itself varies from very high to hi-lo-hi. Over Eastern England there is the possibility of a lo-lo-lo attack profile involving anything from a pair of 'Fencers' to a whole regiment of 'Backfires' or perhaps in the future 'Blackjacks'. They can come by day or by night, in fair weather or in foul. The burden of defence has until now been carried by Phantoms and Lightnings, but this will gradually pass to the Tornado ADV, or as it is known in RAF service, Tornado F.3.

To counter the wide range of threats over such a great area, the air defence Tornado needs a good range and loiter capability, as many on-board kills as can reasonably be carried, the ability to engage multiple targets in quick succession, both at high and low altitudes, and the ability to operate autonomously in the face of heavy ECM. Realistically, the role called for an interceptor rather than an air superiority fighter, and it was as an interceptor that the air defence Tornado took shape. During its gestation period, possible alternatives were evaluated, of which only the Grumman F-14 looked capable of meeting the very stringent requirements. This extremely capable fighter was rejected on cost grounds; Tornado was selected as being at least equal to the F-14 as a fighter, although it lacked the Tomcat's ultra-long range Phoenix missile, at only two thirds the cost of the American aircraft.

By the end of 1985 only one ADV Tornado unit had been formed, No. 229 Operational Conversion Unit at RAF Coningsby, which is equipped with the Tornado F.2.

Tornados would scramble on instructions from Central Operations Centre and be airborne from the crewroom in ten minutes or less, depending on state of readiness. Crews would have a vector, and assume they were going quite some way away. They would make use of AEW or NATO AWACS, which can break the enemy formation down for the ADVs and give them tactical information at long range, so that as the Tornados approach they are already gearing up for the attack.

The pilot will basically do the interceptions while the chap in the back is going to be very much a battle manager, he will be collating all the data from the sensors, radar, datalink, RHWR, and other aids, sifting and considering it, and handing across intercepts to the frontseater. With the combination of an experienced pilot and a less experienced back-seater, a certain amount of discussion would take place with the pilot having more influence over the navigator's decisions.

Tornado ADV aircrew like to fly at a height where they can loiter comfortably and yet see a long way with their radar, using frequency modulated interrupted continuous wave (FMICW), which is basically a more modern pulse-Doppler. With FMICW they are able to see targets further away, and have more information on them. Obviously the Tornado altitude effects a compromise; the higher they fly the more the crew are

Above: The extended nose and slimmer radome of the Tornado F.2 and F.3 greatly improve the looks of the aircraft, but much more important are the new radar and extra internal fuel which lie beneath the skin. The result is an interceptor able to outperform the Phantom while coping with latest-generation ECM.

Below: With afterburners lit and wing flaps still deployed, a Tornado interceptor begins its climb to operating height. Although not intended as an F-15 style dogfighter, the aircraft can out-perform the BAC Lightning – a fighter with an enviable reputation as a 'pilot's aircraft'.

Runway requirements

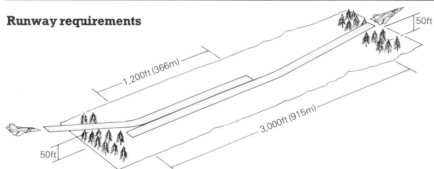

At sea level, Tornado interceptors can comfortably operate out of 3,000ft (915m) airstrips; thanks to the built-in thrust reverser the landing roll is even shorter. NATO planning assumes that Soviet equivalents of the JP233 and MW-1 would be unable to make its runways unusable.

Datalink application

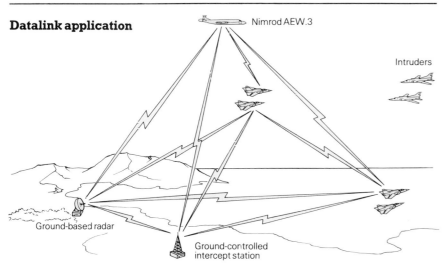

Nimrod AEW.3

Intruders

Ground-based radar

Ground-controlled intercept station

The use of a secure datalink allows Tornado interceptors to share target data with ground-based radar stations, RAF Nimrod AEW.3 and NATO E-3A Sentry airborne early-warning aircraft, or even with other Tornado ADVs. In wartime, of course, an enemy would do his best to jam these data transmissions and degrade the fighters' effectiveness.

Below: The AI24 radar was designed for operation in the face of intense jamming, so it uses a Cassegrain antenna rather than the flat-plate type used in contemporary sets such as the USAF Eagle's APG-63 and the US Navy Tomcat's AWG-9.

Above: With flaps and slats extended, and the horizontal stabilizer at near-full deflection, a Tornado F.2 closes in on the photographic aircraft. The horizontal surface near the top of the fin is an antenna for the ILS glideslope and localizer.

looking at targets which are lower than them. If they assess the threat as being at low level, then they want to see them as far away as possible at low level.

Tornado defenders would obviously be in constant communication with other defence elements with the information displayed on the Plan Position Indicator in the rear cockpit. Aircrews can be given an area on which to concentrate in which case the computer will disregard data outside that to avoid saturation. The radar operates in track-while-scan mode which can track multiple targets while continuing to search for others.

At some point, the Tornado crew would be allocated targets and cleared to go down, either to investigate or to engage; targets would already be on the TAC display and a single target could be selected by the navigator for interception. At the same time, the navigator would give the pilot information on where the others were, to avoid putting themselves into an unhealthy position. Hopefully, the first thing that the target would know about the attack would be when he sniffed the exhaust fumes from the missile, a split second before the big bang!

While the ADV Tornado was intended as an interceptor, other virtues are emerging, as the discerning air show goer can testify. At Farnborough 84 the most spectacular displays were given by the Northrop F-20 and the Mirage 2000; by contrast, the Tornado F.2 display was

just slightly subdued. But as the mischievous gentleman in the BAe chalet said, "Why don't you ask your French and American friends why they don't fly with a full war load. After all, we do!" It was a valid point.

Tornado versus Spitfire

Then, in 1985, a really unusual display team appeared at a number of shows around the country: a Battle of Britain Flight Spitfire flown by Sqn Ldr Paul Day in formation with a Tornado F.2 piloted by the commanding officer of No. 229 OCU, Wg Cdr Rick Peacock-Edwards. The ability of the fast jet to fly formation with a fighter designed some 50 years ago speaks volumes. Wg Cdr Peacock-Edwards commented on the Tornado's handling from the pilot's viewpoint in the following words:

"Anybody who saw my display with the Spitfire this year has seen its ability to turn with the Spitfire, and they will have been left in no doubt as to its turning ability. Despite being designed as a long range interceptor it has a very impressive manoeuvre capability. If we get into a turning fight we will have the wings forward. We've got a variety of manoeuvre devices on the aircraft, and they all work. The rate of roll is superb even with the wings spread, and our sustained turn rate is exceptionally good.

"Tornado is absolutely magnificent; it really does fly beautifully. The controls are light, I think about 30 per cent lighter

than on the GR.1, and they are well harmonized. Supersonic handling qualities are very good; years back I used to fly the Lightning, and that was superb, but this seems to handle just that bit better. When you are manoeuvring around you are always aware that you are supersonic, but Tornado handles so well. . . .

"One of the biggest things about flying this aircraft is that it handles like a fighter. After flying the Phantom it feels like a fighter, and it makes the Phantom feel like a bomber. From what we have seen so far, it out-performs the Lightning, it easily out-performs the Phantom, and at low level it is even a match for the Hawk. It will be a very effective performer in the close combat, multi-bogey arena. In multi-bogey fights these days we've got a big problem with the missile technology and we are moving into the environment where we just point the aircraft and shoot the missiles. In fact, we don't even have to point the aircraft very much.

"Having a back-seater is one of the greatest advantages in close combat and I find him absolutely invaluable. He is a man to keep an eye on whatever is going on around you and especially to keep an eye on your six o'clock.

"If we are in a turning fight and we want to bug out, we simply unload, throttles right forward and wings right back, and she goes like a bomb. She accelerates extremely quickly. We have

got a system called SPILS on the aircraft as well, which gives what amounts to carefree handling. And from the crew point of view, the cockpits are luxurious. In every area it has greater capability than the Phantom. Wing sweep on the F.2 is manual. At the moment we have three settings, which are 25°, 45°, and 67°, the same as the IDS, but we are soon getting a fourth, which will be 58°. With Tornado F.3, the wing sweep will be fully variable and fully automatic.

"In combat the same old rules apply, surprise and survival, especially survival. We prefer to operate in pairs, but we could operate in fours, sixes, or who knows, depending on the threat. Cloud cover is one of those things that we would use a lot depending on the situation, but only when we know that our six is clear. If the opportunity arises it would be a good way to attack because we can stay in there and the enemy is not going to be able to see us."

The abiding impression following visits to both Marham and Coningsby was the undiluted enthusiasm of the aircrews for the Tornado, which is apparently echoed by the Germans and Italians. This impression was reinforced by one man, who, aware that he must sound like a Panavia salesman, saw fit to add, "This is not a load of bull's droppings; we really feel like this!" And from the fighter point of view, if the F.2 is great, the F.3, with all its improvements, will be even better.

Future Development

Panavia is not resting on its laurels: Tornado will serve well into the next century, and will require new weapons and sensors matched to threats still on the drawing board. Our final chapter looks at the new weapons already being developed, the advanced avionics likely to be installed during mid-life updates, and versions of the aircraft which have yet to see service. The Tornado of the future will be a deadlier and stealthier opponent and a valuable complement to Europe's next collaborative venture, the twin-engined European Fighter Aircraft, planned as the future agile air-superiority fighter.

Planned improvements to Tornado fall into two categories. In the short term there are minor modifications to the avionics suite and new types of missile and ordnance, equipment not ready for service when the aircraft was originally delivered. In order to prolong its combat effectiveness, the aircraft will also undergo a mid-life update.

One of the first short-term upgrades, to be introduced on Block 5 aircraft and retrofitted to earlier models, is a package of avionics modifications which will allow German Navy Tornados to carry and launch the Texas Instruments AGM-88 Harm (High-speed anti-radiation missile). An initial batch of 23 rounds has been ordered to allow evaluation trials from Tornado, and West Germany has been offered 866 AGM-88As with spares, test equipment and other support for $390 million. Germany is reported to be considering licence production, but although the UK was offered a licence-production deal in the early 1980s the US Navy is apparently opposed to German production.

Like all pre-1980 anti-radar missiles Harm flies a direct course to the target, and can be countered by shutting down the radar until the missile has passed. In this event Harm has one advantage which earlier weapons lacked – it can continue toward the now-silent target under the control of its inertial navigation system. The latter also acts as a safeguard against the enemy turning on decoy transmitters, since it would detect the seeker's attempt to redirect the missile's flight towards the decoy.

An alternative approach to silencing radars, studied in the US and Germany in the late 1970s, was the harassment drone, a low-cost miniature remotely-piloted vehicle (RPV) able to orbit for long periods above areas of interest searching for hostile signals. Once an emitter was detected, the RPV would switch into a homing mode, entering a diving attack. If the radar switched off, the RPV would break off its attack, climbing away and returning to altitude to recommence a search pattern. This behaviour would continue until the RPV's fuel supply was exhausted.

The harassment drone concept never caught on, but Marconi and BAe kept the idea of a loitering weapon in mind when collaborating in the late 1970s on technology suitable for a next-generation anti-radar missile. The result was the BAe Alarm (Air-Launched Anti-Radiation Missile), a weapon not much larger than Sparrow, and small enough to be carried on Sidewinder style launch rails mounted on the side of a weapons pylon.

In 1983 BAe signed a fixed-price development and production contract worth around £300 million and covering the supply of 750 rounds to the RAF. Current plans assume large-scale export orders, and a total production run of 2,000 rounds. Carry trials of the weapon on Tornado started in early 1985, with flight tests of guided rounds due to begin in the USA early in 1986, leading to a service-entry date of 1987.

The seeker of Alarm is programmed with details of the emitters likely to be encountered, and the threat priority assigned to each. It does not need to be cued by the aircraft's RWR, but can detect and identify its own targets. The seeker will normally be programmed before take-off, but may be updated in flight, a useful capability in the event of the aircraft being diverted to an alternative target.

Below: The Alarm anti-radar missile is scheduled to arm RAF Tornados from 1987: maximum load is nine, as seen here, but a more likely operational load would be two on each inboard wing pylon in addition to the normal strike payload and ECM pods.

Weapon release will take place at low altitude. For attacks against specific threat systems, Alarm can be used in direct-attack mode, flying directly towards the target. In this respect it differs little from earlier weapons. Its unique quality is a secondary indirect mode intended to harass and silence radars operating in a pre-defined area. Being rocket-powered, Alarm cannot cruise over the battlefield the way harassment drones were planned to operate. Instead, the motor lofts the weapon to a height of around 40,000ft (12,000m), where it deploys a parachute and begins a slow descent during which the seeker can carry out an autonomous search for a suitable target.

The signals received by the seeker will be analyzed, then compared with the pre-stored threat data. Once the highest-priority target has been identified – a formidable signal-processing task for a low-cost, throwaway seeker – the parachute will be released, allowing the missile to begin an unpowered dive attack. This must be made with great accuracy, since the weapon's small dimensions restrict the size of warhead which may be fitted.

Above: Aerodynamic model of the ANS supersonic anti-ship missile, one of a number of next-generation weapons now under development that may arm Tornado in the 1990s.

When Alarm is released in direct attack mode the seeker does not need to be locked on before launch. There is a consequent risk that the shot will not result in a kill should the missile fail to lock on or the radar be shut down after launch. During development, it was realized that the two operating modes could be combined, allowing rounds fired in direct mode to switch to indirect if the target is not acquired after a pre-defined interval.

The German Navy has another new missile under development for its Tornado fleet. MBB's Kormoran 2 will have a longer range, better target selection facilities, increased resistance to ECM and an improved warhead, and will be suitable for multiple-launch attacks, while maintenance will be simpler, improving operational availability. First test launches were expected to begin in 1986, leading to series production from 1987-88 onwards.

Mid-life update

By the end of the 1980s Tornado will have begun the process of mid-life updating, receiving the improved avionics, engines and weapons needed to maintain its combat effectiveness into the 1990s and beyond. No details of planned updates had been released by the end of 1985, but it was possible to make some educated guesses.

External changes should be minimal. The pace of aerodynamic development runs at a much slower pace than that of weaponry and avionics, and the most likely major change might be the addition of modest leading-edge root extensions to improve manoeuvrability, plus the addition of fairings to house new sensors.

Replacement of some existing metal components by carbon-fibre substitutes might save weight. An all-composite taileron 17 per cent lighter than the standard unit has already been developed by BAe, and was test-flown in 1982. Any remaining structural work is likely to consist of modifications intended to increase structural strength, either to permit greater take-off weights or to cure any fatigue problems which might have emerged by the late 1980s as operating hours of the Tornado fleet build up.

The engine is unlikely to be changed, but the electromechanical engine-control system fitted to earlier production aircraft will probably be replaced by a full-authority digital engine-control (FADEC) similar to that fitted to the ADV. Such systems allow more precise control of engine and aircraft operation than is possible with conventional hydromechanical or pneumatic technology. The latter incorporate wear-sensitive mechanical components, and flowing-air networks are vulnerable to contamination and corrosion.

Tornado was designed too soon to take advantage of microprocessor technology, but this will almost certainly be introduced during a mid-life update, reducing the size of avionics units and increasing their reliability. Despite the upgrade in computer capacity from the current 64K to 128K already planned, a further improvement is likely. The specification for a next-generation system could involve an increase to at least the 500K already flying in the F/A-18A Hornet, and possibly even more.

Introduction of a MIL-STD-1553 databus would allow a more flexible alternative to installing a massive central computer of 1M capacity or greater – the use of distributed computing. Under this scheme, many of the sensors and other avionic systems would have built-in computer facilities enabling them to tackle their own calculations rather than pass the task over to the main computer. This would require a massive effort to create new software, which could well conform to the latest NATO standards such as MIL-STD-1750 computer architecture and the new ADA programming language.

The displays are obvious candidates for upgrading. The current patterns of CRT display could be replaced by multi-colour units, while the existing HUD could be replaced by a wide-angle design able to present FLIR imagery during all-weather and night attacks. Several UK teams have already tested HUDs of this type.

In its current form, the aircraft lacks the night navigation/attack performance made possible by the USAF's Lantirn FLIR/laser designator, but the RAF has already drawn up ASR 1010 to cover the development of equipment of this type in the UK. In addition to superimposing a thermal image on the view of the external world seen through the HUD, such a system could also be used to cue fire-and-forget missiles.

In order to cope with agile opponents in the Mirage 2000/MiG-29 performance class, Tornado could receive additional air-to-air target tracking aids. The radar could be given a new short-range air-combat mode, and one or both crew members could be provided with helmet sights.

The EW suite will also require updating, but such is the pace in this field that such updating will probably be carried out independently of any formal mid-life programme, being introduced as required by the developing threat. Planned upgrades include new RWRs and jamming systems, and reports that the RAF plans to retrofit the ADV RWR in the IDS were mentioned in the avionics chapter, but there are no reports of a follow-on to Sky Shadow.

In the 1980s, the Cerberus jamming pod carried by Luftwaffe Tornados could be replaced by a new system known as Zeus. Currently under development by AEG Telefunken, this should not be confused with the Marconi system of the same name, the latter being an internal system for the Harrier GR.5. The Zeus system being developed for the Luftwaffe is a pod-mounted jammer of advanced design.

The aircraft's navaids will also be updated. For a start, the existing FIN 1010 inertial system could be replaced by a laser-gyro system. In February 1985 the Bracknell division of BAe Dynamics was given a £1 million contract covering the development of two laser-gyro INS systems for delivery in 1986. If adopted for service, this would be installed on the European Fighter Aircraft (EFA) and retrofitted to Tornado IDS. A new INS could also be supplemented by a Navstar/GPS receiver able to obtain navigation "fixes" from the radio signals emitted by US navigational satellites.

One logical goal of an IDS mid-life update would be to reduce the aircraft's electromagnetic signature by placing greater reliance on passive sensors. A Lantirn-style FLIR would be one step in this direction; another would be to supplement or even replace the terrain-following (TF) radar with BAE's Terprom (Terrain Profile Matching) navigation system. Similar to the Tercom (Terrain Contour Matching) guidance system used by US cruise missiles, Terprom entered flight test in 1979 in a Jetstream trials aircraft. It was then test-flown on an F-16 during a series of trials carried out by General Dynamics, and flight trials are continuing on the F-16 and Tornado, according to BAe.

ASRAAM and ANS

Improvements to the avionics will be matched by the availability of new weapons, including new air-to-air and anti-ship missiles and improved versions of existing air-to-ground ordnance. Many of these armament developments will be the result of international collaborative ventures.

AIM-132 ASRAAM (Advanced Short-Range Air-to-Air Missile) is currently in the early stages of development as NATO's long-awaited Sidewinder replacement, and should enter service in the early 1990s. Being developed by BBG – an international company formed by BAe Dynamics and West German missile manufacturer Bodenseewerk Gerätetechnik – the weapon will also be built in the United States to equip the US forces.

ASRAAM is a wingless missile which derives lift directly from its fuselage. Shorter and fatter than Sidewinder, it is around 8ft (2.5m) long and 6in (15cm) in diameter. It is steered by four aft-mounted cruciform fins, and guided by an infra-red seeker of advanced design plus an inertial reference unit (probably a strap-down flex gyro system or a ring-laser gyro system). The seeker will probably be a three-axis stabilized design able to lock on to targets from any aspect, and having the discrimination to pick out a single target from a close formation.

The missile will have several operating modes. Like most modern IR-homing weapons, it will be able to carry out an autonomous search for targets while still mounted on the launch rail, or may be assigned a target by having its seeker head slaved to the radar antenna of the launch aircraft. Another designating method likely to be adopted for ASRAAM involves slaving the seeker to a helmet sighting system, but by the autumn of 1985 an official requirement for this had yet to be released.

While ASRAAM maintains Tornado's air-combat capability, new air-to-surface weapons will be needed to improve its attack performance. The most exotic of these is probably the Aérospatiale/MBB Anti-Navire Supersonique (ANS), a supersonic successor to the Exocet anti-ship missile. Much faster than existing weapons, ANS should be able to penetrate the improved ship defences of the 1990s.

Pre-development work ended in 1985, with a choice of powerplant expected in 1986. ANS will use an integrated rocket/ramjet: when the solid-propellant charge of the booster motor is exhausted, four externally mounted intakes will be opened and allow air to enter the motor, which will then act as a ramjet. Two alternative designs have been developed – a liquid-propellant Aérospatiale unit and an MBB solid-propellant ramjet using boron compounds.

ANS will have a maximum range similar to that of Exocet, but will be much faster, with a cruise speed of around Mach 2 at low level, rising to Mach 2.5 at altitude. For most of its flight, the round will follow inertial guidance; terminal homing will probably be by means of an Electronique Serge Dassault Super Adac active-radar seeker. According to

Alarm indirect attack mode

To overcome the standard counter to anti-radar missiles – simply shutting down until the threat has passed – Alarm's indirect attack mode involves boosting the missile to around 40,000ft (12,000m), where a parachute is deployed to enable the seeker to search for targets during the descent.

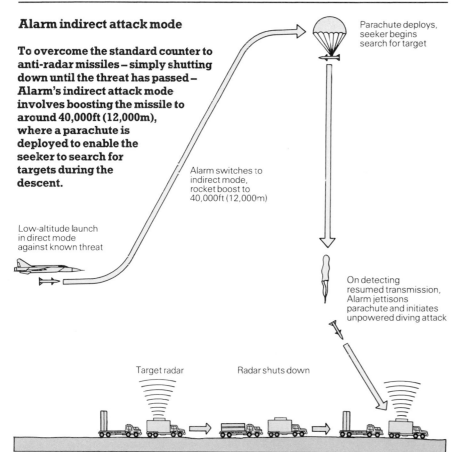

Parachute deploys, seeker begins search for target

Alarm switches to indirect mode, rocket boost to 40,000ft (12,000m)

Low-altitude launch in direct mode against known threat

On detecting resumed transmission, Alarm jettisons parachute and initiates unpowered diving attack

Target radar   Radar shuts down

some reports, the weapon will fly high-g terminal manoeuvres in order to confuse defensive systems such as short-range SAMs and point-defence guns. MBB is developing a semi-armour-piercing warhead.

Operational evaluation firings of ANS are expected to begin in 1992. The initial version of the missile is expected to be the air-launched weapon, with the ship-launched variant following within six months or so. This schedule could be speeded up if an urgent need for the weapon should emerge.

New air-to-ground weapons
Improvements will also be needed to Tornado's air-to-ground weaponry, and both the UK and West Germany have programmes in hand. The antitank munitions carried by the MW-1 dispenser are unguided – the weapon simply saturates the target area in order to obtain hits on enemy armour– but German engineers are believed to be developing terminally guided submunitions.

Following the demise of the VJ291 off-boresight air-to-ground weapon in 1982, the UK opted to develop an improved version of the BL755 cluster bomb as an interim anti-armour weapon. Another adaption of the BL755 resulted in the Hades area-denial bomb, which carries 49 of the HB876 mines used in JP233, but it is not clear whether this will be adopted for use on Tornado.

These weapons still require the launch aircraft to pass close to or even overfly the target area. Even in the 1980s, this is already a hazardous undertaking, so next-generation systems will incorporate some degree of stand-off capability. A number of weapons are already under study; one or more could arm Tornado IDS in the 1990s.

LOCPOD (Low-Cost Powered Off-axis Dispenser) is a proposed NATO-standard air-to-ground guided weapon intended to dispense submunitions. It will probably use inertial guidance, and have a range of 8.5-17nm (16-32km).

France and Germany are collaborating on a weapon in the same performance class. Known as Apache/CWS, this will be a modular dispenser about 13ft (4m) long, around a ton in weight and fitted with fold-out wings of 8.2ft (2.5m) span. The weapon would be available in jet-powered, rocket-powered or un-

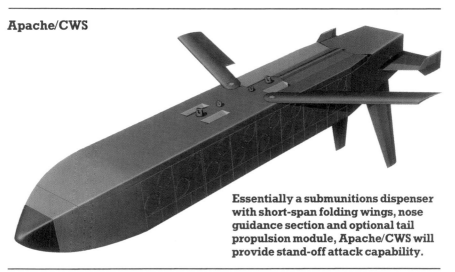

Apache/CWS

Essentially a submunitions dispenser with short-span folding wings, nose guidance section and optional tail propulsion module, Apache/CWS will provide stand-off attack capability.

powered forms, with ranges from 6.5nm (12km) to 25nm (50km). The payload would consist of specialized submunitions such as antitank or anti-personnel mines which would be scattered over an area around 3,000ft (1,000m) long and 1,100ft (350m) wide. The UK's Air Staff Target 1238 calls for the development of a stand-off anti-armour dispenser for service in the late 1990s.

For missions requiring a greater stand-off range, RAF and Luftwaffe Tornados will probably carry the Long Range Stand-Off Missile (LRSOM), which has been studied by two international industrial teams headed by Boeing and General Dynamics respectively. Competitive feasibility studies of this subsonic 320nm (600km) range weapon were under way in 1985 with the goal of creating operational hardware by the early 1990s.

Another international venture is Vebal, originally known as Vebal/Syndrom, which is under development by MBB and Westinghouse. Vebal is a self-contained anti-armour weapon packaged in a pod which may be carried under the wing of a Tornado, A-6 or A-7. Armoured targets are detected by three sensors whose combined output will give a good chance of activating the weapon in the presence of genuine targets only. An IR linescan unit locates heat sources on the battlefield and a laser scanner measures target size, while a millimeter wave radiometer responds only to large metal objects.

When an armoured formation is detected, the pod releases 21 KB 44 antitank submunitions, a weapon already used by the sideways-firing MW-1.

Harm and Alarm will not meet all NATO anti-radar missile (ARM) requirements – many air forces see the need for a smaller weapon around the size of Sidewinder which could be fired at short range to deal with immediate tactical threats such as point-defence radars and SAMs. The UK, for example, has drawn up Air Staff Target 1240 covering a weapon of this type. Belgium, Canada, West Germany, Italy, the Netherlands, the UK and the USA signed an MoU in late 1984 covering the development of a definitive Short-Range Anti-Radiation Missile (SRARM). One possible solution to this requirement might be to mate the airframe and propulsion system of the AIM-132 ASRAAM with a new passive radar seeker.

ADV upgrade
A mid-life upgrading similar to that scheduled for Tornado IDS is planned for the ADV. In the late 1980s the aircraft will be retrofitted with the Hughes AIM-120 AMRAAM missile and a JTIDS data link. These modifications will involve the installation of a MIL-STD-1553B digital data bus as part of the avionics suite.

Developed to replace the AIM-7 Sparrow missiles of the USAF and USN, AMRAAM has a higher velocity and an extended performance envelope, plus a fire-and-forget capability which allows

the simultaneous engagement of several targets following a multiple launch. The US services require more than 24,000 rounds over the next decade, 17,217 for the USAF and 7,257 for the USN.

AMRAAM was to have entered service on the USAF's F-16s in FY 1986, but in January 1985 the programme was re-scheduled, extending its full-scale development phase by 22 months. A production decision was postponed until the summer of 1985, and will not be taken until the DoD is satisfied that costs have been brought under control. Procurement is now due to begin in FY86, allowing the weapon to enter service on the F-16C in mid-1988.

In the meantime, potential users are also looking at alternatives to AMRAAM, presumably as a hedge against cancellation. The USAF is reported to have examined an upgraded version of Sparrow which would be able to meet some of the AMRAAM mission requirements, while the US Navy has been investigating a tail-controlled version of Sparrow. The current weapon has fixed tail fins, and is guided by moving the cruciform wings: by making the wings fixed, and using modern actuator technology to create a miniature fin-control system able to wrap around the nozzle of the Sparrow rocket motor, designers would be able to free the space currently used by the current and relatively bulky wing actuator system. This could be used to give the weapon a larger rocket motor, and thus a longer range. For the moment, this is aimed at naval SAM applications only, says Raytheon, which is still firmly backing the AIM-120. Despite this, tail-control technology and a modern seeker using microminiaturized electronics could be used to create a "Super Sparrow" for air-to-air use.

Like Raytheon, the UK government is firmly backing AMRAAM, since the US missile is due to re-arm the Tornado ADV force and the Royal Navy's Sea Harrier FRS.2 fighters. As a result, it has shown little interest in a proposed AMRAAM-class indigenous missile – the Sky Flash 90. Seen as a possible collaborative programme with Sweden, this could enter service in 1990 to arm the planned JAS 39 Gripen fighter.

Sky Flash is aerodynamically identical with Sparrow, but the proposed new version could embody minor aerodyna-

Above: Linescan 4000 infra-red image of Luton Airport at ×4.5 magnification. Taken in darkness from 800ft (250m), with hot areas showing black, the image allows such details as floodlights (1), full oil (2) and aviation fuel (3) tanks, street lights (4), and car parking (5) and fuel bowser (6) areas to be pinpointed even at night.

Right: Reconnaissance equipment installed for trials on a Tornado in September 1985. No optical cameras are used: the fairing below the fuselage houses the Linescan 4000 miniaturized IR line-scanner, while a window on each side is provided for a pair of sideways-looking thermal imaging sensors.

mic modifications while a Marconi active radar seeker would give fire-and-forget capability similar to that of AMRAAM. The UK is reported to be planning a modest update of the RAF's Sky Flash missiles, replacing the existing Aerojet rocket motor with a new unit of Royal Ordnance design known as Hoopoe. This could be used in Sky Flash 90; it would improve general performance, but maximum range would still be below that of the US missile.

Sky Flash 90 could receive a degree of UK Government support as a safeguard against AMRAAM cancellation. BAe studies have suggested that the weapon could find a ready market in the 1990s with air arms which need a weapon of this performance class but which cannot afford the Hughes missile or would not be cleared by the US Government to purchase the AIM-120. Italy is also planning an AMRAAM-class missile. Known as Idra (Hydra), this will be based on Aspide, Selenia's Sparrow look-alike, and will have an active radar seeker.

IFF and JTIDS

During its lifetime, the Tornado ADV will have to be equipped with a new IFF interrogator compatible with the NATO Identification System (NIS), the planned replacement for the Mk 10/12 IFF system. Until this new system enters service, the ADV will be unable to make full use of AMRAAM's ability to engage multiple targets beyond visual range.

The European NATO Allies – with the exception of France – wanted any new IFF system to operate in E/F band (2-4GHz), but the USAF, which has the largest number of IFF systems to replace, was determined to stay with D-band (1-2GHz) in order to reduce the retrofitting problem. This impasse lasted for six years, but in 1985 the West German Defence Ministry finally indicated that it would be prepared to accept a D-band system, provided that this incorporates a radar mode.

The radar mode will allow the radar pulse emitted by the ground or airborne surveillance sets to interrogate the airborne IFF beacons. In the current system, this can be done only by specialized interrogators operating on dedicated IFF frequencies, and by allowing the radar's powerful main pulse to interrogate beacons the new IFF system should be usable at much longer ranges. The final system will also use spread-spectrum technology to make its D-band transmission hard for an enemy to detect.

Tornado ADV will also be retrofitted with the US-developed JTIDS jam-resistant data link. Singer Kearfott has received a contract from the UK for the supply of terminals to be installed in the Tornado ADV, the Nimrod AEW.3 early-warning aircraft and the UK Air Defence Ground Environment (UKADGE) radar system. JTIDS will allow data to be exchanged between individual Tornados, Nimrod and E-3A Sentry AEW aircraft, and ground-based radars. Having received data on fresh targets, Tornado will be able to correlate these with its own radar and IFF-derived targets and tracks, displaying the result within six seconds.

More powerful engines may be retrofitted during the aircraft's career. With its eye on the proposed European Fighter Aircraft (EFA) project, Turbo-Union has already run demonstration engines offering 35 per cent more thrust than current RB199s. The UK has insisted that the new engine planned for use in the EFA must be dimensionally compatible with the Tornado F.2, allowing it to be retrofitted into the F.3 fleet, and BAe's Experimental Aircraft Prototype uses two RB199 Mk 104s.

New variants

In addition to updates, Panavia has also studied new versions of Tornado. The first of these is a reconnaissance version of the IDS intended to equip the RAF's two reconnaissance squadrons. This version is immediately recognizable by the presence of an optical window in the side of the fuselage associated with the aircraft's internally-mounted sensors. Most tactical reconnaissance aircraft carry conventional cameras, but the RAF's recce Tornado has an all-electronic sensor installation consisting of a BAe sideways-looking infra-red (SLIR) and a Linescan 4000 unit. Both are roll-stabilized.

The SLIR system is based on components created by the UK Thermal Imaging Common Module System (TICMS), and uses UK-developed SPRITE (Signal PRocessing In The Element) detector technology. The detector is cooled by a split-Stirling Cycle cryogenic cooling system able to operate for long periods of time. Linescan 4000 is smaller and lighter than previous units, and also uses SPRITE and Stirling-Cycle technology.

Signal processing and video recording are handled by equipment developed by Computing Devices. Using a cockpit-mounted display, the back-seater is able to watch the imagery being gathered in real time or replay the videotape recording. The results appear in the form of a high-definition thermal image which may be magnified or enhanced at the touch of a switch. Flight trials of the sensors started in a Tornado GR.1 during the late summer of 1985.

The second new variant is an electronic combat and reconnaissance (ECR) version intended to meet a West German air force requirement for such an aircraft to supplement its existing RF-4 Phantoms. The Luftwaffe currently operates around 80 Phantoms in the reconnaissance role: these carry daylight and IR cameras and sideways looking radars, but no armament or EW equipment, and are reaching the end of their useful lives, so the service would like to buy a batch of 40 Tornado ECR in order to supplement and eventually replace the ageing Phantoms. Italy is also a possible ECR user, and could order up to 12.

Work on the ECR started early in 1984 and Panavia proposals were submitted to the West German Defence Ministry in January 1985. Other aircraft considered

for this role included modified versions of the F-16 and F-18. Tornado ECR is based on the standard IDS variant, most of the changes being confined to the avionics suite. One of the two 27mm cannon would be deleted, making room for an internally mounted sensor designed to allow the aircraft to locate threat emitters. Also mounted internally would be IRIS, incorporating forward and sideways-looking IR sensors.

Two pod-mounted systems would also be carried. One would be the MBB recce pod, described in the Avionics chapter, developed for the German Navy and the Italian Air Force. The other will carry a jamming system, probably a repackaged version of the USAF/USN ALQ-99 which equips the EF-111A and EA-6B EW aircraft.

ECR development is expected to take 2-3 years, with funding required from 1986 onwards and total cost of procurement (40 aircraft) estimated at DM 3,700 million. If ordered, these aircraft would form part of an anticipated seventh production batch of at least 60 aircraft.

Long anticipated as a top-up order to replace attrition losses, Batch 7 was made neccessary by the Omani and Saudi orders, and the need to replace aircraft originally destined for the RAF but diverted to the Gulf. The first of the RAF's recce Tornados were due to be delivered in March 1986, but these airframes could become candidates for delivery to the Gulf, making the recce aircraft part of Batch 7. Although an order for this new batch had not been placed by the end of 1985, BAe had already begun ordering long-lead items such as castings and forgings for the additional aircraft.

It is possible that yet another variant could eventually see light of day. Consideration has been given to creating a new export-orientated Tornado variant combining the strike capability of the IDS with the airframe of the ADV. This project may be designated Tornado International, and could be selected by Oman for its anticipated follow-on buy.

Below: ECR Tornado model configured for defence suppression, with Harm and Sidewinder missiles, fuel tanks and ECM pods; internal systems will include IR, radar location and data processing equipment.

ECR Tornado stores options

Among the external stores envisaged for the electronic combat and reconnaissance role are both current and future weapons and EW equipment.

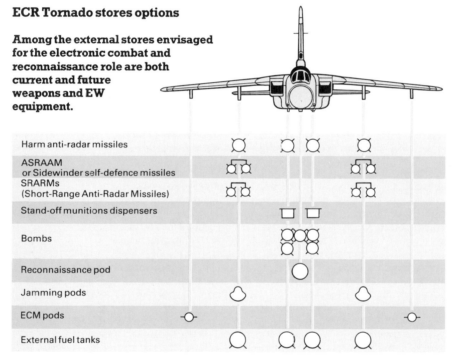

Harm anti-radar missiles		⊡	⊡ ⊡	⊡	
ASRAAM or Sidewinder self-defence missiles		⬠⬠		⬠⬠	
SRARMs (Short-Range Anti-Radar Missiles)		⬠⬠		⬠⬠	
Stand-off munitions dispensers			▢ ▢		
Bombs			◯◯◯ ◯◯◯		
Reconnaissance pod			◯		
Jamming pods		◠		◠	
ECM pods	⊸				⊸
External fuel tanks		◯	◯◯	◯	

Specifications

PANAVIA TORNADO

DIMENSIONS	IDS (RAF GR.1)	ADV (RAF F.2)
Length	54ft 10¼in (16.72m)	59ft 3in (18.06m)
Height	19ft 6¼in (5.95m)	18ft 8in (5.70m)
Wing span (swept)	28ft 2½in (8.60m)	28ft 2½in (8.60m)
Wing span (spread)	45ft 7½in (13.91m)	45ft 7in (13.90m)

WEIGHTS		
Empty	31,065lb (14,091kg)	31,500lb (14,290kg)
Max external fuel	12,900lb (5,850kg)	12,800lb (5,806kg)
Max weapon load (approx)	19,840lb (9,000kg)	18,740lb (8,500kg)

TAKEOFF WEIGHTS		
Clean, max internal fuel	45,000lb (20,411kg)	47,500lb (21,540kg)
Maximum	60,000lb (27,215kg)	61,700lb (27,986kg)

PERFORMANCE		
Max speed (hi/clean)	Mach 2.2	Mach 2.27
Max speed (lo/clean)	Mach 1.2	Mach 1.2
Max speed (lo/external stores)	Mach 0.9	Mach 0.9
Max g	7.5	7.5
Takeoff distance	2,500ft (760m)	2,500ft (760m)
Landing roll	1,200ft (366m)	1,200ft (366m)

COMBAT RADII		
Hi-lo-lo-hi	750nm (1,390km)	N/A
Combat air patrol (2hr loiter)	N/A	300-400nm (560-740km)
Ferry range	2,100nm (3,890km)	2,100nm (3,890km)

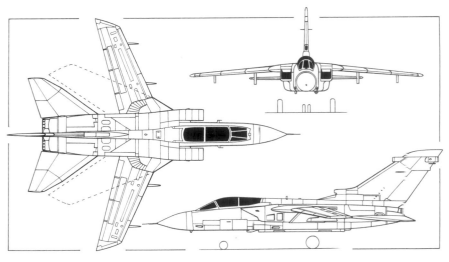

Tornado IDS (RAF GR.1)

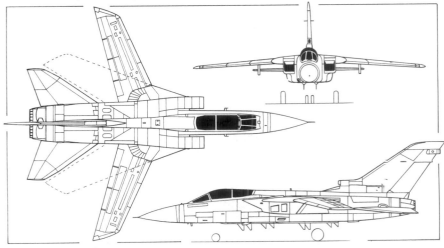

Tornado ADV (RAF F.3)

Production Plan

Note: Batch 7 order expected during 1986; no announcement made by end January 1986.

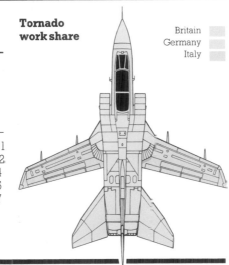

Tornado work share

- Britain
- Germany
- Italy

Batch no.	Date ordered	No. of aircraft	Customers				Delivery Period
			UK		Germany	Italy	
			IDS	ADV	IDS	IDS	
1	November 1976	43	23	3	17	0	Nov 1979-May 1981
2	May 1977	110	55	0	40	15	Feb 1981-Dec 1982
3	June 1979	164	68	0	68	28	Oct 1982-Mar 1984
4	August 1981	162	53	18	64	27	Feb 1984-Oct 1985
5	August 1982	171	20	52	70	29	May 1985-Jun 1987
6	January 1984	155	0	92	63	0	Jun 1987-Jul 1989
TOTALS		**805**	**219**	**165**	**322**	**99**	

Time Scale

This chart compares the pace of development of Tornado with that of contemporary US and French fighters; see page 14 for a discussion of the implications.

	1967	1968	1969	1970	1971	1972	1973	1974	1975	1976	1977	1978	1979	1980	1981	1982
TORNADO		First MoU signed	Project definition	Programme go-ahead				Prototype 1st flight		Production decision			Prod a/c 1st flight	Deliveries begin (IDS)		
F-14	RFPs issued		Grumman selected	First flight		Deliveries begin										
F-15	RFPs issued		Contract awarded			First flight		Deliveries begin								
F-16						YF-16 ordered		YF-16 1st flight		F-16A/B ordered	Prod a/c 1st flight		Deliveries begin			
F/A-18						YF-17 ordered		YF-17 1st flight		F/A-18 ordered			F/A-18 1st flight	Deliveries begin		
MIRAGE 2000									Development approved			First flight				Deliveries begin

Picture credits

Endpapers: A. Johnson **Title page:** RAF Coningsby **Page 2/3:** (centre left) Panavia; (bottom left and centre right) BAe **4/5:** (centre left) Dassault-Breguet; (remainder) BAe **6/7:** (top left) MBB; (remainder) BAe (both) BAe **9:** (top) Panavia; (bottom) Aeritalia **10:** (top) BAe; (bottom) Panavia **11:** (top) MBB; (centre) Panavia **12/13:** (top left and right) BAe; (bottom left and right) Panavia **14/15:** (all) BAe **16:** (top) BAe; (bottom) Panavia **18/19:** (top left) Robert F. Dorr; (centre) Rolls-Royce; (bottom right) Aeritalia **20:** Robert F. Dorr **21:** BAe **22/23:** (bottom left) Turbo-Union; (remainder) Rolls-Royce **24/25:** (centre left) Rolls-Royce; (top right) BAe; (bottom left and right) Turbo-Union **26/27:** (bottom right) Fiat Aviazione; (remainder) Rolls-Royce **28/29:** (bottom) A. Johnson; (remainder) Panavia **30/31:** (all) Panavia **32/33:** (both) Panavia **34:** MBB **36/37:** (top left and right) Panavia; (centre) MBB; (bottom) BAe Dynamics **39:** (both) Panavia **40/41:** (top and centre left) MBB; (top and centre right) BAe; (bottom) Hunting Engineering **42:** (top) Panavia; (centre) MBB **43:** (top); BAe (bottom) BAe Dynamics **44:** (left) BAe; (right) MBB **45:** BAe **46/47:** (top left and right) Panavia; (top right) BAe; (bottom right) Robert F. Dorr **48/49:** (top left) BAe; (centre and bottom left) Robert F. Dorr; (remainder) Jeremy Flack/Aviation Photographs International **50/51:** (top left) Robert F. Dorr; (remainder) Panavia **52:** (both) Panavia **53:** BAe **54/55:** (top left) MBB; (top right) Jeremy Flack/API; (remainder) BAe **56/57:** (top left) Panavia; (bottom right) MBB; (remainder) BAe **58/59:** (top left and right) BAe; (bottom left) Panavia; (centre right) GEC Avionics **60/61:** (top left) MBB; (bottom left) BAe; (top right) BAe Dynamics **62/63:** (top left and bottom right) MBB; (remainder) BAe Dynamics